( ) human rights *first*

In Pursuit of Justice

Prosecuting Terrorism Cases in the Federal Courts

2009 Update and Recent Developments

Richard B. Zabel
James J. Benjamin, Jr.

July 2009

About Us

Human Rights First believes that building respect for human rights and the rule of law will help ensure the dignity to which every individual is entitled and will stem tyranny, extremism, intolerance, and violence.

Human Rights First protects people at risk: refugees who flee persecution, victims of crimes against humanity or other mass human rights violations, victims of discrimination, those whose rights are eroded in the name of national security, and human rights advocates who are targeted for defending the rights of others. These groups are often the first victims of societal instability and breakdown; their treatment is a harbinger of wider-scale repression. Human Rights First works to prevent violations against these groups and to seek justice and accountability for violations against them.

Human Rights First is practical and effective. We advocate for change at the highest levels of national and international policymaking. We seek justice through the courts. We raise awareness and understanding through the media. We build coalitions among those with divergent views. And we mobilize people to act.

Human Rights First is a non-profit, nonpartisan international human rights organization based in New York and Washington D.C. To maintain our independence, we accept no government funding.

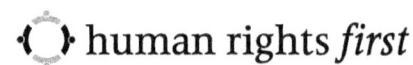

◀ ◯ ▶ human rights *first*

Headquarters	Washington D.C. Office
333 Seventh Avenue	100 Maryland Avenue, NE
13th Floor	Suite 500
New York, NY 10001-5108	Washington, DC 20002-5625
Tel.: 212.845.5200	Tel: 202.547.5692
Fax: 212.845.5299	Fax: 202.543.5999

www.humanrightsfirst.org

Preface

As the Obama Administration takes steps to shut down the Guantánamo Bay detention facility, the heated debate over when and how to prosecute suspected terrorists continues. Some commentators have asserted that bringing accused terrorists to the United States to face trial and incarceration poses a danger to American communities. Others have argued for the creation of a new, untested legal regime to preventively detain and/or prosecute persons suspected of complicity in terrorism. Often missing from this debate is the fact that the federal courts are continuing to build on their proven track record of serving as an effective and fair tool for incapacitating terrorists.

Because of the importance of resolving the question of when and how to try and detain terrorism suspects to our national security, our legal culture, and our standing in the world, we have updated our May 2008 report, *In Pursuit of Justice: Prosecuting Terrorism Cases in the Federal Courts*, to include cases and developments from the past year. Together, we believe *In Pursuit of Justice* along with this 2009 Report, *In Pursuit of Justice: Prosecuting Terrorism Cases in the Federal Courts—2009 Update and Recent Developments* (hereinafter "2009 Report"), are the most comprehensive analysis ever undertaken of criminal cases arising from terrorism that is associated—organizationally, financially, or ideologically—with self-described "jihadist" or Islamist extremist groups like al Qaeda. And we hope these reports will continue to help focus the debate on these important issues. In total, we have analyzed 119 cases with 289 defendants. Of the 214 defendants whose cases were resolved as of June 2, 2009 (charges against 75 defendants were still pending), 195 were convicted either by verdict or by a guilty plea. This is a conviction rate of 91.121%, a slight increase over the 90.625% conviction rate reported in May of 2008.

Our research also found:

■ The statutes available to the Department of Justice for the prosecution of suspected terrorists continue to be deployed forcefully, fairly, and with just results.

■ Courts are authorizing the detention of terrorism suspects under established criminal and immigration law authority and, now through the time-tested common law system, are delimiting the scope of military detention to meet the demands of the current circumstances.

■ The Classified Information Procedures Act (CIPA), although subject to being improved, is working as it should: we were unable to identify a single instance in which CIPA was invoked and there was a substantial leak of sensitive information as a result of a terrorism prosecution in federal court.

■ The *Miranda* requirement is not preventing intelligence professionals from interrogating prisoners, and recent court decisions have not interpreted *Miranda*, even in the context of foreign law enforcement interrogations, as a bar to criminal prosecution.

- Prosecutors are able to make use of a wide array of evidence to establish their cases.

- Convicted terrorists continue to receive stiff sentences.

- The Federal Bureau of Prisons has been detaining accused and convicted hardened terrorists in U.S. prisons on a continuous basis since at least the early 1990s without harm to the surrounding communities.

In sum, the federal courts, while not perfect, are a fit and flexible resource that should be used along with other government resources—including military force, intelligence gathering, diplomatic efforts, and cultural and economic initiatives—as an important part of a multi-pronged counterterrorism strategy. In contrast, the creation of a brand-new court system or preventive detention scheme from scratch would be expensive, uncertain, and almost certainly controversial. The analysis of additional data from the past year confirms our conclusion from *In Pursuit of Justice* that the criminal justice system has been and should continue to be an important tool in confronting terrorism.

The primary authors of this 2009 Report are Richard B. Zabel and James J. Benjamin, Jr., partners in the New York office of Akin Gump Strauss Hauer & Feld LLP. They, along with a dedicated team at Akin Gump, devoted much hard work and many long hours to prepare this report on a pro bono basis. Members of the Akin Gump team include Joseph Sorkin, Jessica Budoff, and Amit Kurlekar, who provided indispensable leadership and assistance throughout the process, as well as Peter Altman, Daniel Chau, Russell Collins, Jane Datillo, Ryan Donohue, Monica Duda, Jonathan Eisenman, Daniel Fisher, Jessica Herlihy, Leslie Lanphear, Sherene Lewis, Isabelle Liberman, Kathleen Matsoukas, Andrew Meehan, Elizabeth Raskin, Gary Thompson, Ashley Waters, and Elizabeth Young. Although Akin Gump is proud of the firm's commitment to pro bono work, the views expressed in this 2009 Report include those of the primary authors and Human Rights First; they are not the views of Akin Gump as a whole or other Akin Gump attorneys.

Table of Contents

I.
Introduction and Overview

In May 2008, Human Rights First released *In Pursuit of Justice: Prosecuting Terrorism Cases in the Federal Courts*.[1] Based on a comprehensive review of more than 120 actual prosecutions dating back to the 1980s, *In Pursuit of Justice* concluded that the criminal justice system is well-equipped to handle a broad variety of criminal cases arising from terrorism that is associated—organizationally, financially, or ideologically—with self-described "jihadist" or Islamist extremist groups like al Qaeda. The roster of cases chronicled in *In Pursuit of Justice* ranges from blockbuster trials against hardened terrorists who planned or committed grievous acts around the world to complex terrorism-financing prosecutions and "alternative" prosecutions based on non-terrorism charges such as immigration fraud, financial fraud, and false statements. Many of these cases have been preemptive prosecutions focused on preventing and disrupting terrorist activities. *In Pursuit of Justice* acknowledged that terrorism prosecutions can present difficult challenges, and that the criminal justice system, by itself, is not "the answer" to the problem of international terrorism, but it found that the federal courts have demonstrated their ability, over and over again, to effectively and fairly convict and incapacitate terrorists in a broad variety of terrorism cases.

In the year since *In Pursuit of Justice* was issued, there have been a number of important developments. On his second day in office, President Obama issued Executive Orders mandating the closure of the Guantánamo Bay detention facility within one year and establishing a Detention Policy Task Force to examine U.S. policy regarding the detention, interrogation, and trial of individuals suspected of participating in terrorism.[2] The effort to close Guantánamo has proved to be fraught with difficult policy and political choices and, more generally, our country continues to wrestle with the complex problems posed by the scourge of terrorism. Apart from Guantánamo, our military forces remain deployed in Iraq and Afghanistan; the situation in Pakistan is unstable; and radical Islamist groups continue to threaten our national interests in many corners of the globe.

In this environment, there is broad consensus that the government must continue to deploy all available resources—including military, intelligence, diplomatic, economic, and law enforcement tools—to address the threat of international terrorism. It seems self-evident that, as an important part of an integrated counterterrorism strategy, the government must have a reliable, stable system in place for prosecuting accused terrorists when such prosecutions are appropriate in light of the evidence and the law. The question remains as to where, and under what set of rules, terrorism prosecutions should occur.

President Obama has expressed a preference for trying accused terrorists in federal court whenever possible, but in two separate public statements in May 2009, he signaled that the government expects to prosecute some detainees in reconstituted military commissions with revised procedural rules.[3] The President also noted that the government intends to develop "clear, defensible and lawful standards" for longer-term detention of individuals who cannot be prosecuted but who the government believes pose an unacceptably high risk to release.[4]

The President offered these remarks against the backdrop of a vigorous and ongoing debate about how the government should prosecute terrorists. Some commentators have agreed with the conclusion of *In Pursuit of Justice* that the justice system is equal to the task of handling a broad swath of terrorism prosecutions, while others have posited that the federal courts are unable to do so effectively—or that the risk of a prosecution that does not yield a conviction is unacceptable—and that, as a result, Congress should authorize a new "national security court" with lower evidentiary standards or other prosecution-friendly features that would supplant the Article III courts in some terrorism cases.[5]

This update to *In Pursuit of Justice* takes a renewed look at the capability of the federal courts to handle terrorism cases based on developments in the year since the White Paper was written. As was the case with the White Paper, this 2009 Report is grounded in actual data and experience rather than abstract or academic theories. We have set out to identify, examine, and analyze the terrorism cases that have been prosecuted in federal court in the past year, including cases that were pending when *In Pursuit of Justice* was issued a year ago. In addition, outside the body of traditional criminal prosecution case law, we have examined emerging case law sketching the contours of permissible law-of-war detention in the terrorism context. Although we might have missed some cases, we have continued the development of substantial data that, we believe, provides a sound foundation for examining the adequacy of the court system to cope with terrorism cases.

This 2009 Report begins with an updated presentation of data about terrorism prosecutions, including statistics through June 2, 2009. The 2009 Report then addresses some of the key legal and practical issues that were presented in international terrorism cases within the past year. As was the case with the White Paper, we address topics as diverse as the scope and adequacy of criminal statutes to prosecute alleged terrorists; the sufficiency of existing legal tools to detain individuals suspected of involvement in terrorism; and means of dealing with classified evidence. We also address the courts' experience with evidentiary issues in terrorism cases; recent developments regarding the applicability of the *Miranda* rule in overseas interrogations; observations about sentencing proceedings in terrorism cases; and information confirming that the federal prisons have been able to maintain a high degree of security over the accused and convicted terrorists confined within them.

We believe that the experience with terrorism cases in the past year strongly supports the conclusion in the White Paper that prosecuting terrorism defendants in the court system generally leads to just, reliable results and does not cause serious security breaches or other problems that threaten the nation's security. As a result, we continue to believe that the need for a new "national security court" is not apparent, especially given the numerous false starts and problems associated with the prior failed effort to establish military commissions at Guantánamo.[6] Nor is it evident that the case has been made for a brand-new legal regime to preventively detain individuals without charge—especially when one considers the potentially damaging effects such a momentous step could have on our legal system and culture. At the same time, as in the White Paper, we continue to believe that there are several important qualifications on our conclusion about the efficacy of the Article III courts to handle terrorism cases—namely that the justice system is not, by itself, "the answer" to the problem of terrorism; that terrorism cases can pose significant burdens and strains on the courts; and that the court system is not infallible and will stumble from time to time.

It must be emphasized that the efficacy of the criminal justice system in any particular case ultimately depends on the evidence. We commend the government for finally undertaking a detailed case-by-case review of the evidence regarding each of the Guantánamo detainees, and we strongly believe that the disposition of those cases should be guided, first and foremost, by the evidence. For many individuals, we anticipate that the evidence will be sufficient to support federal-court prosecutions; but for some individuals, that may not be the case. It remains to be seen, and may never be known, how much damage to the viability of criminal prosecutions was caused by the years of delay, among other things, that occurred before a comprehensive assessment of admissible evidence took place.

Assuming sufficient evidence is available to bring a prosecution, we have observed that the most difficult challenges come up when the potential criminal case arises out of or substantially overlaps with military or intelligence operations. The military services and our intelligence agencies are proud institutions with deeply rooted traditions and practices, and they do not always coexist easily with the norms and legal requirements of the criminal justice system. But experience shows that when the government decides to bring terrorism prosecutions in federal court, the different arms of the Executive Branch are capable of working together in

order to ensure that the cases proceed properly. The key is to institutionalize this sort of coordination so that it can be replicated and in effect becomes "muscle memory" among the relevant agencies and departments. We hope that the current Detention Policy Task Force will provide a framework for better coordination in the future among the Department of Justice, intelligence agencies, and the military.

Another significant challenge is that of resources. Managing large terrorism cases is expensive and labor-intensive for all participants, including prosecutors, defense lawyers, the courts, and the prison system. It is critical that sufficient resources be devoted on all sides so that cases are handled correctly.

As in the White Paper, we recognize that views on the subject matter of this report continue to be charged and will vary. We acknowledge the difficulty of finding definitive answers and reaching consensus on a subject that intertwines fundamental questions of security, justice, and what our Nation exemplifies to the world. We believe that a serious and objective analysis of the subject must rely on facts, and that idealized theories and doctrinaire approaches are not useful. We hope that by extending our findings and analysis we can advance the ongoing—and critically important—debate about how to reconcile our commitment to the rule of law with the imperative of assuring security for all Americans.

II.
The Data on Cases Prosecuted in Federal Court

As we discussed in *In Pursuit of Justice*, we have sought to ground our analysis, as much as possible, in actual data and experience rather than abstract or academic theories. In order to make observations and draw conclusions about the criminal justice system's approach to terrorism prosecutions and ability to manage them effectively, we built a data set of relevant terrorism cases and examined the court system's handling of everything from pre-trial detention to sentencing. In this 2009 Report, we have updated our quantitative analysis to reflect activity between December 31, 2007, and June 2, 2009, in the cases that were pending when the White Paper was issued. We have also used the screening and search methods outlined in the White Paper to add additional cases to our data set that were filed between September 12, 2001, and June 2, 2009. In some cases, this meant revisiting previously screened cases to determine whether new information about those cases made them appropriate for inclusion in our data set. As a result, we added 7 cases to our data set that were filed between September 12, 2001, and December 31, 2007, but that were not included in the White Paper.

As in *In Pursuit of Justice*, we have defined "terrorism cases" to encompass prosecutions that are related to Islamist extremist terrorist organizations such as al Qaeda or individuals and organizations that are ideologically or organizationally linked to such groups.

Although other categories of cases, including prosecutions of domestic militias or violent international groups such as the FARC in Colombia, might reasonably be considered to be aimed at "terrorism," we have restricted our definition as outlined above in light of the legal, intelligence, and security concerns that are thought to make al Qaeda and similar groups a special threat to our national security. In building our data set of terrorism cases, we have attempted to capture prosecutions that seek criminal sanctions for acts of terrorism, attempts or conspiracies to commit terrorism, or providing aid and support to those engaged in terrorism. We have also sought to identify and include prosecutions intended to disrupt and deter terrorism through other means, for example, through charges under "alternative" statutes such as false statements, financial fraud, and immigration fraud. We have included these cases if the indictment or information charges that the criminal activity was connected to terrorist organizations or activities or if there are other assertions or evidence in the case that concretely demonstrate the government's belief that there is such a connection in the particular case. As in *In Pursuit of Justice*, we have limited our analysis to criminal prosecutions; we have not sought to analyze military tribunals or non-criminal immigration proceedings.

As noted above and in the White Paper, the process of identifying and gathering terrorism cases is inevitably an imperfect one, and our data set almost certainly does not contain the full universe of prosecutions involving Islamist extremist terrorist groups and individuals and organizations that are ideologically, financially, or organizationally linked to them. However, we believe that our collection of cases is sufficiently robust and representative to permit us to identify certain recurring factual and legal circumstances in terrorism prosecutions, analyze the judiciary's response to those circumstances, and draw conclusions based on that analysis.

Terrorism Prosecutions Filed and Defendants Charged, 9/12/2001 – 6/2/2009

As in the White Paper, our analysis in this 2009 Report is based on both pre- and post-9/11 cases, and many pre-9/11 cases play a significant role in our consideration of the practical and legal issues presented in terrorism prosecutions. However, for purposes of our quantitative analysis, we have restricted our data set to cases filed after September 11, 2001. In Appendix A, we include a list of all of the terrorism cases that we have identified and examined, including both pre- and post-9/11 cases. Cases added for the first time in this 2009 Report are denoted with an asterisk.

As shown in Figure 1, we have identified 119 cases filed since September 11, 2001, that meet the criteria outlined above and in the White Paper. There were 289 defendants charged in those cases.

Figure 1: Total Number of Terrorism Cases and Defendants

	Cases	Defendants
Total	119	289

As compared to the data presented in the White Paper, these figures represent an 11% increase in the number of cases filed and a 12% increase in the number of

defendants charged over the comparable figures for December 31, 2007.[7] For purposes of tabulating the number of cases filed and defendants charged, we have counted an individual charged as a defendant in more than one case as a defendant in each case. If a prosecution is dismissed in one jurisdiction and related charges are pursued in a separate jurisdiction, we generally have treated that circumstance as a single case in the second jurisdiction, with data from the prior prosecution noted as relevant procedural background.[8]

Figure 2 shows the cases in our data set broken down by the year of filing and by the number of defendants first charged by year of the charging instrument.

Figure 2: Number of Terrorism Cases and Defendants by Year[9]

	Cases	Defendants
2001	21	35
2002	23	60
2003	18	71
2004	14	31
2005	14	26
2006	12	22
2007	11	35
2008	2	2
Jan.–June 2009	4	7

These figures indicate that while there was a general declining trend in the number of cases filed in each succeeding year since 2001, there was an increase in the number of defendants charged in 2007 over the three prior years and there has been an increase in new cases filed in the first five months of 2009 over the number of cases filed in 2008. In assessing the year-over-year data, 2008 is a clear outlier, with a dramatically lower number of new cases filed and new defendants charged as compared to all other full years since 9/11. Although one could speculate as to the reasons for this apparent anomaly, the empirical data, standing alone, do not provide an answer. The data in Figure 2 is shown graphically on page 8 in Figures 5 and 6.

Terrorism Prosecutions Filed by Jurisdiction

Figures 3 and 4 summarize the geographical distribution of cases in our data set. The leading jurisdictions, both by number of cases and number of defendants, continue to be the Eastern District of Virginia, the Southern District of New York, and the Eastern District of New York. This data is shown graphically on pages 10-11 in Figures 9, 10, and 11.

Figure 3: Top Jurisdictions by Cases Filed

		Cases	Defendants
1	E.D. Va.	22	34
2	S.D.N.Y.	18	52
3	E.D.N.Y.	9	19
4	D.N.J.	6	13
5	N.D. Ill.	5	9
6	D. Mass.	5	8
7	E.D. Mich.	3	19
7	S.D. Fla.	3	14
7	D. Ariz	3	4
7	D. Conn.	3	4
7	S.D. Ohio	3	3
7	S.D. Tex	3	3
7	S.D. Cal.	3	8
7	N.D. Ohio	3	6
7	D.D.C	3	13
20 jurisd.		2 or fewer	80 total
Total		119	289

Figure 4: Top Jurisdictions by Defendants Charged

		Defendants	Cases
1	S.D.N.Y.	52	18
2	E.D. Va	34	22
3	E.D.N.Y.	19	9
4	E.D. Mich.	19	3
5	N.D. Tex.	16	2
6	S.D. Fla.	14	3
7	D.N.J.	13	6
7	D.D.C.	13	3
8	M.D. Fla.	11	2
9	N.D. Ill.	9	5
25 jurisd.		8 or fewer	46 total
Total		289	119

Pre-Trial Detention

Of the 289 defendants in our data set, 45 have yet to be brought into custody because they are fugitives, currently are subject to extradition proceedings or cannot be extradited, are deceased, or for some other reason. Another 7 defendants are legal entities rather than individuals, and bail information was not available for 10 individuals. Thus, 227 individual defendants have been arrested and have had a bail determination made by the court.

Of these 227 defendants, 157 were ordered detained without bail and 82 were released on conditions. These figures reflect a detention rate of approximately 69%, slightly higher than the 67% detention rate reported in the White Paper for cases through December 31, 2007.[10] In the 2009 Report, we counted 12 defendants in each category (i.e., ordered detained and released on bail) because either they were initially detained but later were granted release on conditions, or initially were granted release on conditions and later had bail revoked. Figure 13 on page 12 presents graphically the data showing pre-trial detention compared to release on conditions.

Figure 5: Number of Terrorism Cases Filed, 9/12/2001 – 6/2/2009

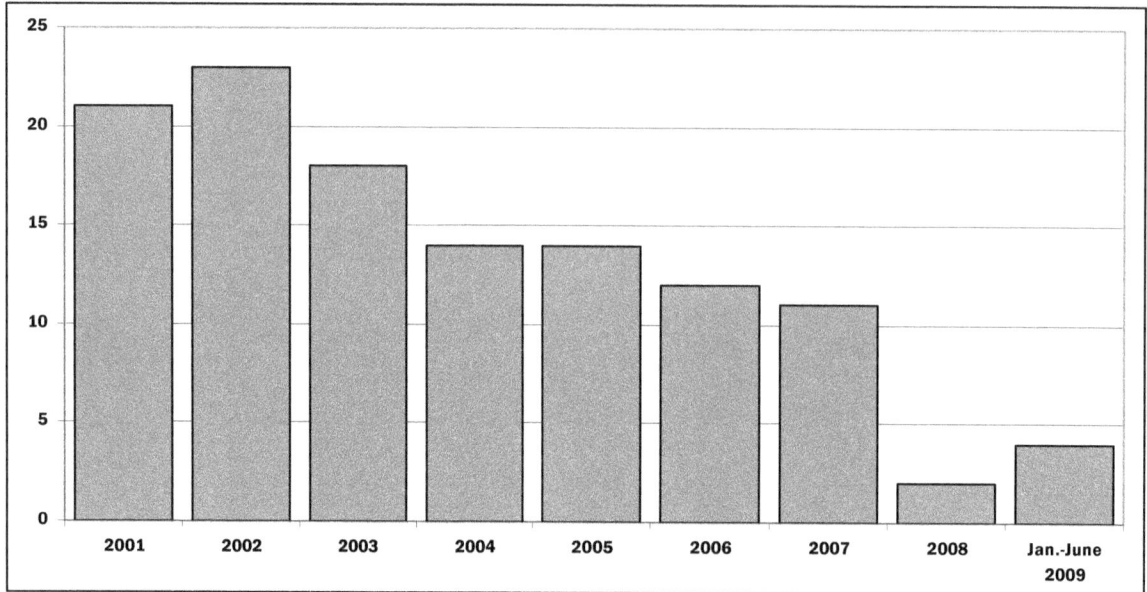

Figure 6: Number of Defendants Charged in Terrorism Cases Filed, 9/12/2001 – 6/2/2009

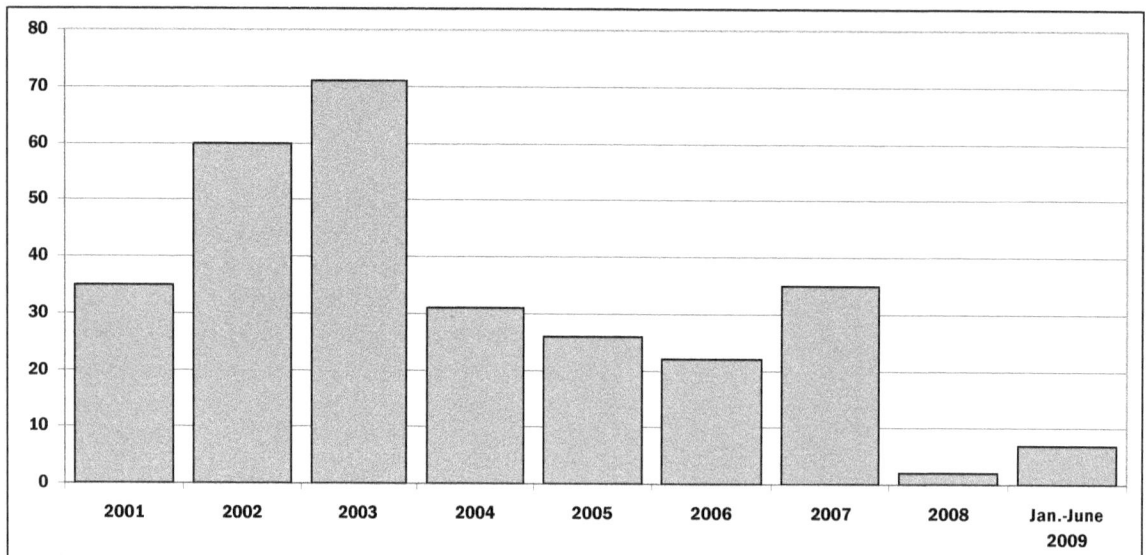

Outcomes in Terrorism Prosecutions

Of the 289 defendants in our data set, 75 still have charges pending against them. This leaves 214 defendants who have had charges against them "resolved," which we define to mean that the charges were terminated either by conviction at trial or in a plea agreement, or by acquittal or dismissal of charges following arraignment.[11] As compared to the data reported in the White Paper for cases through December 31, 2007, these figures reflect an approximately 34% increase in the number of defendants who have had all terrorism charges resolved.[12]

Of the 214 defendants who have had charges resolved, 195 were convicted of at least one count, either by a verdict of guilty after trial or by a guilty plea. And of those 214, 19 defendants have been acquitted of all charges or have had all charges against them dismissed following arraignment.[13] However, it must be emphasized that many of the defendants in this latter category did not ultimately "win" in any normal sense of the word. For example, in cases such as *Arnaout*, *Benkhala*, *Hammoudeh*, and *Elmardoudi*, even though the defendant obtained an acquittal or dismissal of the charges that were originally filed, the government subsequently brought new charges and ultimately won a conviction and lengthy sentence or an order of removal.[14] Further, even if a defendant obtains an acquittal or dismissal and is not re-prosecuted on new criminal charges, the government may transfer the defendant into immigration detention pending removal from the United States.[15]

Figure 7 shows the conviction data for the defendants whose cases have been resolved using the definition set forth above. The same data is shown graphically in Figures 14 and 15 on page 12. The conviction rate of 91.121% represents a slight increase from the rate of 90.625% that was reported

in *In Pursuit of Justice* for cases through December 31, 2007. *See In Pursuit of Justice*, at 26.

Figure 7: Outcomes in Terrorism Cases, 9/12/2001 – 6/2/2009

Defendants	289	
Charges still pending	73	
Charges resolved	214	
Convicted of any charge	195	91.121%
-Convicted at trial	67	31.308%
-Guilty plea	128	59.813%
Acquitted of all charges or all charges dismissed	19	8.878%

Figure 8 summarizes the sentencing data for defendants who have been convicted of at least one offense and, at the time of writing this 2009 Report, had been sentenced.

Figure 8: Sentencing Data From Terrorism Prosecutions, 9/12/2001 – 6/2/2009

Total defendants sentenced	171
Defendants sentenced to imprisonment (excluding probation or time served)	151
Defendants receiving no additional prison term (i.e., probation or time served)	20
Defendants sentenced to a term of life imprisonment	11
Average term of imprisonment (excluding life sentences)	100.98 Months (8.41 Years)
Median term of imprisonment	58 Months (4.83 Years)
Median term of imprisonment, excluding defendants receiving no additional time	69 months (5.75 Years)

Figure 9: Number of Terrorism Cases Filed
by Jurisdiction, 9/12/2001 – 6/2/2009

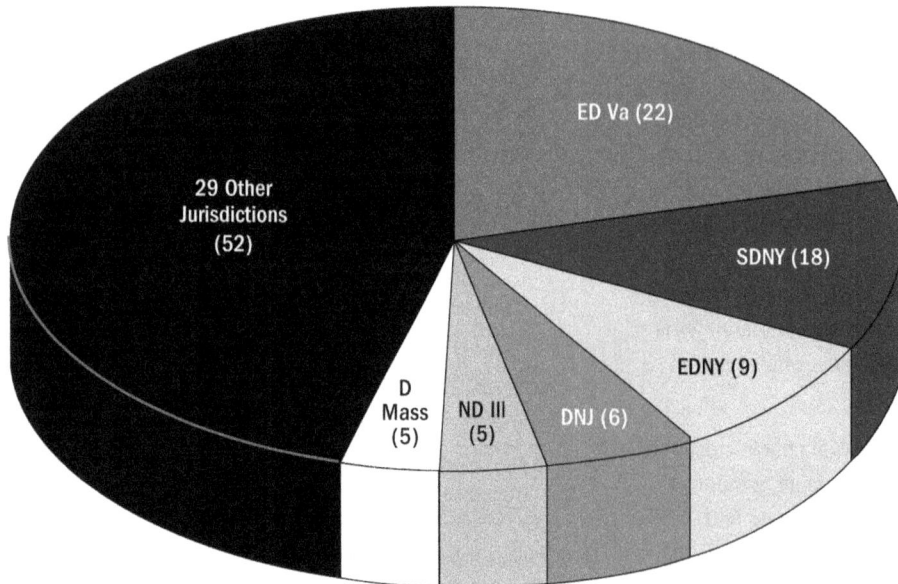

29 Other Jurisdictions (52)

ED Va (22)

SDNY (18)

EDNY (9)

D Mass (5)

ND Ill (5)

DNJ (6)

Figure 10: Number of Defendants
Charged in Terrorism Cases by Jurisdiction,
9/12/2001 – 6/2/2009

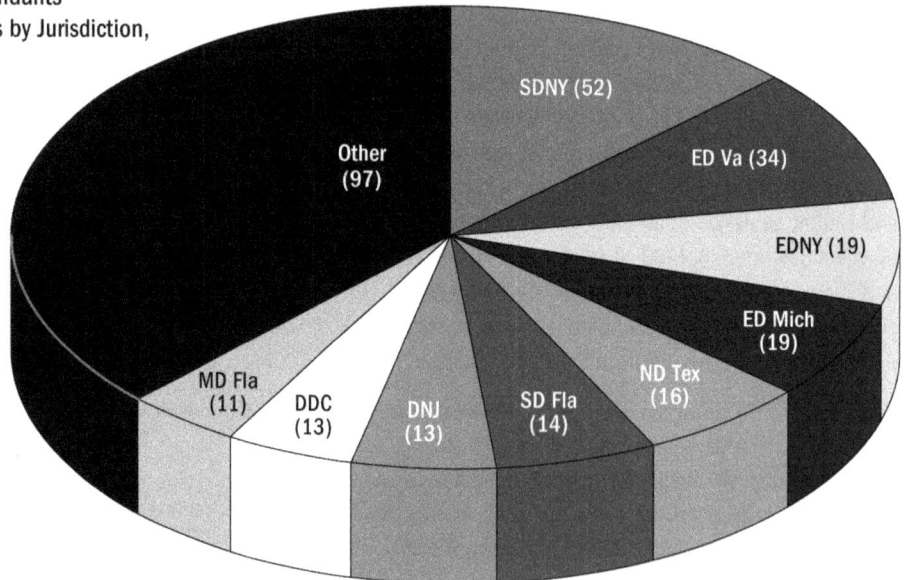

Other (97)

SDNY (52)

ED Va (34)

EDNY (19)

ED Mich (19)

ND Tex (16)

SD Fla (14)

DNJ (13)

DDC (13)

MD Fla (11)

This data is consistent with the sentencing information reported in the White Paper. There was virtually the same rate of imprisonment (89% in the White Paper for cases through December 31, 2007 versus 88% in this 2009 Report for cases through June 2, 2009), with an increase in the number of life sentences (5 in the White Paper and 11 in the 2009 Report) and virtually no change in the average term of imprisonment, excluding life sentences (100.71 months in the White Paper and 100.98 months in this 2009 report).[16]

Offenses Charged in Terrorism Prosecutions

Figure 12, on page 12, shows the statutes most commonly charged against defendants in cases within our data set. A single defendant may be counted multiple times in this chart, once for each statute that he is alleged to have violated. As we noted in the White Paper, although the most commonly charged statutes in our data set are the federal aiding-and-abetting statute, 18 U.S.C. § 2, and the federal

conspiracy statute, 18 U.S.C. § 371, we have omitted these statutes from the table because they are always accompanied by substantive offenses, and because we feel there are limited useful inferences to be drawn from the frequency of these charges.

The most commonly charged substantive offenses in our data set continue to be the material support statutes, 18 U.S.C. §§ 2339A and 2339B. The rest of the list remains largely the same, with the addition of 18 U.S.C. § 2332, killing a U.S. national, and the narcotics distribution and importation conspiracy statutes, 21 U.S.C. § 846, and 21 U.S.C. § 963, respectively.

The table also shows conviction data for these statutes using the methodology we outlined in the White Paper. *See In Pursuit of Justice*, at 28. As we noted in the White Paper, we believe the most important measure is whether the prosecution secured a conviction on any charge against the defendant; the precise statute of conviction is often, though not always, of lesser significance.

Figure 11: Number of Cases Filed by Year, Selected Jurisdictions (9/12/2001 – 6/2/2009)

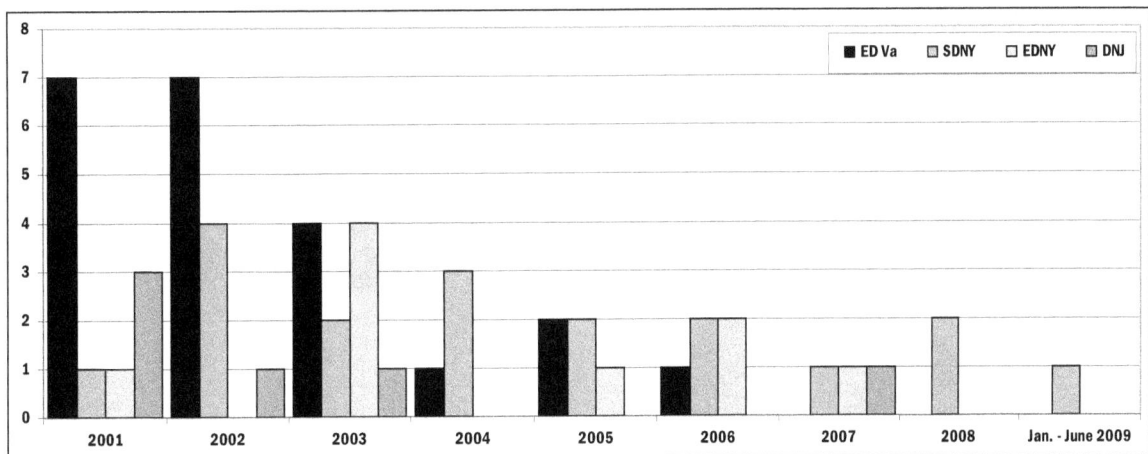

Figure 12: Table of Offenses Charged and Outcomes

	Offense		Defts	Defts with charge resolved	Defts convicted of the specific charge	Defts convicted of any offense
1	18 U.S.C. § 2339B	Material support	83	69	40	57
2	18 U.S.C. § 2339A	Material support	60	47	33	37
3	50 U.S.C. §§ 1701-1706	IEEPA	53	38	26	30
3	18 U.S.C. § 1956	Money laundering	53	37	28	34
4	18 U.S.C. § 924	Weapons charge	45	32	20	29
5	18 U.S.C. § 1001	False statements	42	35	21[17]	31
6	18 U.S.C. § 956	Conspiracy to commit murder	29	17	9	14
7	21 U.S.C. § 846	Controlled substances	26	21	10	19
7	18 U.S.C. § 2332	Killing of U.S. national	26	11	6	11
8	18 U.S.C. § 1962	RICO	25	18	12	16
9	21 U.S.C. § 963	Controlled substances	24	18	12	16

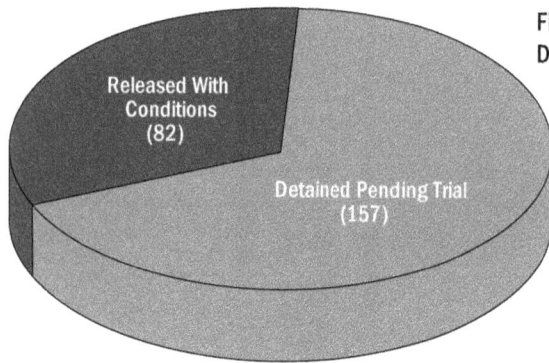

Figure 13: Number of Defendants Detained vs. Released on Conditions

Released With Conditions (82)

Detained Pending Trial (157)

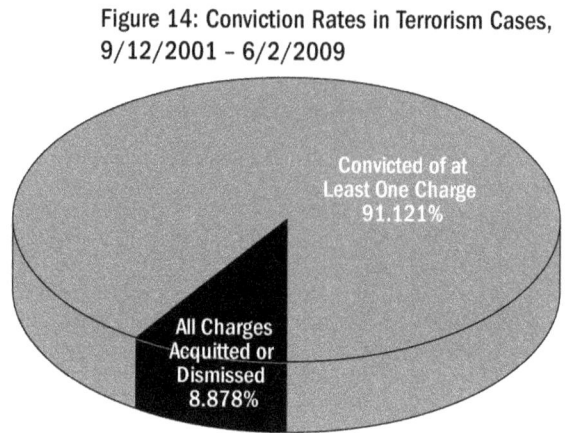

Figure 14: Conviction Rates in Terrorism Cases, 9/12/2001 – 6/2/2009

Convicted of at Least One Charge 91.121%

All Charges Acquitted or Dismissed 8.878%

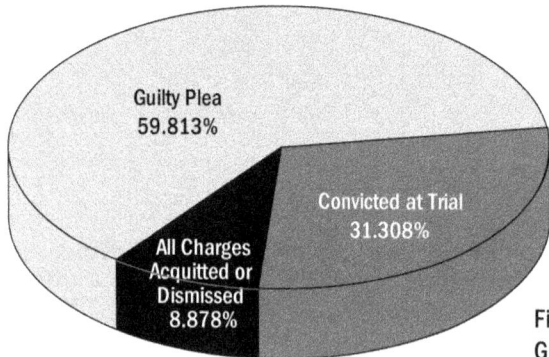

Guilty Plea 59.813%

Convicted at Trial 31.308%

All Charges Acquitted or Dismissed 8.878%

Figure 15: Conviction Rates in Terrorism Cases, Guilty Plea vs. Trial, 9/12/2001 – 6/2/2009

III.
Recent Developments in Material Support Law and the Emergence of Narco-Terrorism Prosecutions

In *In Pursuit of Justice*, we catalogued and analyzed the broad array of federal criminal statutes that have been invoked against accused terrorists. As that discussion made clear, Congress has given prosecutors a formidable arsenal of criminal statutes to deploy in terrorism prosecutions. The list of available charges ranges from specially tailored terrorism offenses to generally applicable crimes such as murder to "alternative" charges such as false statements or financial fraud. In particular, as described at some length in *In Pursuit of Justice*, the statutes criminalizing "material support" of terrorist activities or organizations, 18 U.S.C. §§ 2339A and 2339B, have been among the most effective for the Department of Justice. In the past year, the government has successfully invoked those statutes in a number of important terrorism prosecutions. In the following discussion, we outline some of the significant material support prosecutions of the past year. We also describe the advent of a new and potentially powerful tool for prosecutors, a 2006 statute criminalizing narcotics offenses that are carried out to support terrorism.

A. Material Support Statutes (18 U.S.C. §§ 2339A and 2339B)

The original material support statute, 18 U.S.C. § 2339A, makes it a crime to provide "material support," which is defined to include money, property or services, lodging, training, false identification, communications equipment, personnel (including oneself), weapons or lethal substances, explosives, transportation, safe houses, facilities, or expert advice or assistance, knowing that the support is to be used by someone else in connection with a range of offenses including murder, kidnapping, and the violation of terrorism statutes. 18 U.S.C. § 2339A. As we noted in *In Pursuit of Justice*, § 2339A "can be likened to a form of terrorism aiding and abetting statute." *In Pursuit of Justice*, at 32. Section 2339B, enacted two years after § 2339A, has a slightly different focus. It prohibits the provision of material support to groups, including al Qaeda and the Taliban, that have been designated as foreign terrorist organizations by the State Department. 18 U.S.C. § 2339B. In total, almost half the terrorism cases we surveyed since 9/11 have included charges for offenses under § 2339A or § 2339B.[18] In the past year, material support cases have demonstrated the wide breadth of conduct that these statutes encompass—from cases involving sleeper terrorists to individuals setting up jihad training camps in the United States to individuals providing broadcasting services for a terrorist organization's television station.

Perhaps the highest-profile material support case of the past year is that of Ali Saleh Kahlah al-Marri. As chronicled in *In Pursuit of Justice*, al-Marri underwent a circuitous and heavily litigated eight-year journey from the criminal justice system, where he was originally charged shortly after 9/11 with financial fraud, false identity, and false statement crimes; to the naval brig in South Carolina, where he was detained without charge in military custody for more than five and a half years as an "enemy combatant"; and then back to the criminal justice system in February 2009 to face criminal charges of violating § 2339B based on his close ties to al Qaeda. *In Pursuit of Justice*, at 73-74; *see also* Indictment, *United States v. al-Marri*, No. 09-cr-10030 (C.D. Ill. Feb. 26, 2009) (Dkt. No. 3). In April 2009, al-Marri pled guilty to conspiracy to violate § 2339B, admitting in connection with his guilty plea that: (1) he conspired with Khalid Sheikh Mohammed to work for al Qaeda; (2) pursuant to that conspiracy, he attended terrorist training camps from 1998 to 2001; (3) Mohammed instructed him to enter the United States as a sleeper agent no later than September 10, 2001; (4) he enrolled at Bradley University as a pretext for residing in the United States; and (5) he spent considerable time researching the manufacture of poison gases, learning the kind of information that is taught in "advanced poisons courses" given at terrorist training camps. Plea Agreement and Stipulation of Facts, *al-Marri* (C.D. Ill. Apr. 30, 2009) (Dkt. No. 22). Under the terms of his plea agreement, al-Marri faces a maximum sentence of fifteen years' imprisonment. *Id.* at 3.[19]

In May 2009, in another prominent material support case, a Southern District of New York jury convicted Oussama Kassir of violating the material support statutes based on his role in running a terrorist training camp in Bly, Oregon (at which he taught students hand-

to-hand combat and discussed plans to kill truck drivers and hijack their cargo to fund terrorist operations) and for setting up websites instructing how to "build bombs and make poisons." Indictment, *United States v. Mustafa*, No. 04-cr-00356 (S.D.N.Y. Feb. 6, 2006) (Dkt. No. 6); Jury Verdict, *Mustafa* (S.D.N.Y. May 12, 2009) (reflecting conviction on eleven counts of Indictment, including seven material support counts). Kassir's sentencing has been set for September 9, 2009. Order, *Mustafa* (S.D.N.Y. May 13, 2009) (Dkt. No. 91). And in other recent cases, four defendants have pled guilty to material support counts based on various acts to support Islamist extremist terrorism. *See* Superseding Information, *United States v. Ahmed*, No. 07-cr-00647 (N.D. Ohio Jan. 15, 2009) (Dkt. No. 129) (charging conspiracy to violate § 2339A based on defendants' extensive planning to harm U.S. forces in Iraq and Afghanistan); Plea Agreement as to Zubair Ahmed, *Ahmed* (N.D. Ohio Jan. 15, 2009) (Dkt. No. 132); Plea Agreement as to Khaleel Ahmed, *Ahmed* (N.D. Ohio Jan. 15, 2009) (Dkt. No. 133); Press Release, U.S. Dep't of Justice, Chicago Cousins Plead Guilty to Conspiracy to Provide Material Support to Terrorists (Jan. 15, 2009)[20]; *see also* Indictment, *United States v. Iqbal*, No. 06-cr-01054 (S.D.N.Y. June 20, 2007) (Dkt. No. 42) (Count Two charges violation of § 2339B based on defendants' alleged broadcasting of programming from Hezbollah's television station Al Manar); Judgment, *Iqbal* (S.D.N.Y. Apr. 27, 2009) (Dkt. No. 111) (reflecting sixty-nine month sentence for both defendants pursuant to guilty plea to Count Two of indictment).

In the past year, the government has also achieved successes in material support prosecutions where it had encountered problems previously. In the third trial in Miami of the "Liberty City Six" (originally the "Liberty City Seven" who were accused of planning to blow up the Sears Tower and selected federal buildings), following two prior mistrials, the government was able to obtain material support convictions against five of the six defendants. Jury Verdicts, *United States v. Batiste*, 06-cr-20373 (S.D. Fla. May 12, 2009) (Dkt. Nos. 1291-96). The outcome of the Liberty City Six trial may be seen as an illustration of the significance of the material support charge because, in a case fraught with difficulties, the government fared much worse with its two *non-material support* counts against the Liberty City Six, gaining convictions on its felony explosives count against only two of the six defendants and on its seditious conspiracy count against only one of the six defendants. *See id.*

Similarly, in the past year, the government finally succeeded in its material support prosecutions of the Holy Land Foundation ("HLF") and five of its officers in federal court in Texas. As discussed in *In Pursuit of Justice*, the first HLF trial, in the fall of 2007, ended in a hung jury on some counts and acquittals on others, but with no convictions against any of the defendants. *In Pursuit of Justice*, at 37. A year later, however, the government retried six defendants (two remain at large), and this time secured material support convictions against each one. Jury Verdict, *United States v. Holy Land Foundation for Relief & Dev.*, 04-cr-00240 (N.D. Tex. Nov. 24, 2008) (Dkt. No. 1250). HLF was sentenced to a year of probation and subjected to joint and several liability with the individual defendants for a $12.4 million criminal forfeiture. Judgment, *Holy Land Foundation* (N.D. Tex. May 29, 2009) (Dkt. No. 1297). And the five individual defendants have been sentenced, with each defendant subjected to fifteen years in prison for the material support offenses. Judgments, *Holy Land Foundation* (N.D. Tex. May 28-29, 2009) (Dkt. Nos. 1293-95, 1298-99). Four of the five individual defendants were sentenced on other offenses as well, with the longest sentence totaling sixty-five years. *Id.*

Courts, meanwhile, have by and large continued to uphold the material support statutes against constitutional challenges. *See, e.g., United States v. Chandia*, 514 F.3d 365, 371 (4th Cir. 2008) (upholding

§ 2339B against First Amendment freedom of association and vagueness challenges); *United States v. Warsame*, 537 F. Supp. 2d 1005, 1013-22 (D. Minn. 2008) (upholding § 2339B against First Amendment freedom of association, free speech, overbreadth and vagueness challenges, as well as Fifth Amendment vagueness challenge); *United States v. Taleb-Jedi*, 566 F. Supp. 2d 157, 173-85 (E.D.N.Y. 2008) (upholding § 2339B against First Amendment freedom of association and overbreadth challenges and Fifth Amendment absence of personal guilt and vagueness challenges); *United States v. al-Kassar*, 582 F. Supp. 2d 488, 498 (S.D.N.Y. 2008) (upholding § 2339B against challenge that it fails to satisfy Fifth Amendment due process requirement of personal guilt); *United States v. Amawi*, 545 F. Supp. 2d 681, 683-85 (N.D. Ohio 2008) (upholding § 2339A against First Amendment overbreadth and Fifth Amendment vagueness challenges).

The government suffered a setback, however, in its material support prosecution of Hassan Abu Jihaad. *See United States v. Abu Jihaad*, 600 F. Supp. 2d 362, 401-02 (D. Conn. 2009) (granting defendant's Motion for Judgment of Acquittal as to charges under § 2339A). The government alleged that while Abu Jihaad was serving aboard a U.S. Navy destroyer in 2001, he "disclosed classified information regarding the movement of the Fifth Fleet Battle Group, which included the aircraft carrier, the *U.S.S. Constellation*, to individuals in London associated with Azzam Publications, an organization that the Government alleged supported violent Islamic jihad," with the knowledge or intent that "the information he disclosed would be used to kill United States nationals." *Id.* at 364. In March 2008, a jury found Abu Jihaad guilty of two separate offenses—(1) improperly disclosing national security information in violation of 18 U.S.C. § 793(d) and (2) providing material support to terrorists in violation of § 2339A—based on Abu Jihaad's alleged disclosure. *Id.* With particular respect to the material support charge, the government had alleged in its indictment that Abu

Jihaad's disclosure of intelligence constituted provision of a "physical asset" or "personnel" under § 2339A. *Id.* at 394.[21]

After trial, however, the court threw out the material support conviction, reasoning that the government had not provided sufficient evidence that Abu Jihaad's sharing of intelligence constituted giving Azzam Publications (Azzam) either a "physical asset" or "personnel." *Id.* at 394-402. (The court upheld the jury's verdict as to the other charge under § 793(d). *Id.* at 384-94.) In particular, the court ruled that the government could only secure a conviction on the "physical asset" predicate if it showed that Abu Jihaad had intended to pass the information on to Azzam in a tangible medium (i.e., a floppy disk). *Id.* at 394-96. Similarly, the court reasoned that in order to show that Abu Jihaad was providing himself as "personnel" by giving information to Azzam, the government needed to prove additional facts establishing that Abu Jihaad was more broadly putting himself at Azzam's service, and not merely providing information "on a whim . . . on one occasion, not knowing if Azzam wanted it and without any pre-disclosure or post-disclosure communication with Azzam about the information." *Id.* at 401-02 ("In those circumstances . . . it would be linguistically odd to describe that lone, voluntary act as making personnel available to Azzam.").

At first blush, *Abu Jihaad* could be seen as a case that exposed a dangerous gap in the conduct covered by the material support statutes: specifically, one could consider the provision of intelligence as something that should indisputably constitute material support, and could find troubling both the result in *Abu Jihaad* and the court's statement that "providing information alone to Azzam [is] an act that was not directly prohibited by § 2339A[.]" *Id.* at 401. For two reasons, however, we do not believe that the result in *Abu Jihaad* is indicative of any fundamental flaw in the material support laws. First, if another case like Abu Jihaad's arises, the government could choose a different predicate of

material support on which to base its case. For instance, rather than casting a disclosure like Abu Jihaad's as the provision of "property" or "personnel," the government could argue that the intelligence constitutes any of at least three other categories of material support under § 2339A: (1) "intangible" property, (2) a "service," or (3) "expert advice or assistance" derived from the defendant's "specialized knowledge" that he gained as an enlisted person in the U.S. armed forces. 18 U.S.C. § 2339A(b).[22]

Second, even if the current statutory definition of "material support" does not encompass the providing of intelligence, there is no reason why this omission is set in stone; Congress can simply react to the *Abu Jihaad* case as it did to the *Humanitarian Law Project* cases, *see In Pursuit of Justice*, at 35, and amend the definition to include the giving of intelligence. In other words, if the *Abu Jihaad* case has indeed exposed a gap in the coverage of § 2339A, that gap should be addressed by Congress, as it is inconceivable that Congress would intend for the disclosure of intelligence to be left unaddressed. In short, even where gaps might temporarily exist in the reaches of sweeping statutes like §§ 2339A and 2339B, there is no evidence that the array of statutes available in the criminal justice system as a whole has irremediable gaps that would allow terrorist activity to go unpunished.[23]

B. Narco-Terrorism Statute (21 U.S.C. § 960a)

From the mid-1990s until they were removed from power in late 2001, the Taliban ruled Afghanistan based on a strict and oppressive version of Sha'ria. *See, e.g.*, John F. Burns, *Stoning of Afghan Adulterers: Some Go To Take Part, Others Just Watch*, N.Y. Times, Nov. 3, 1996, at 18.[24] Since being deposed, the Taliban have carried out a brutal insurgency in Afghanistan, and more recently in Pakistan, punctuated by suicide bombings, improvised explosive devices, shootings, and kidnappings for which they have claimed credit. *See, e.g.*, John Ward Anderson, *Kabul Bus Bombing Kills 30*, Wash. Post, Sept. 30, 2007, at A23[25] (reporting Taliban assertion of responsibility for a suicide bombing aboard an Afghan National Army bus killing at least thirty people and injuring twenty-nine and detailing other terror tactics); *Taliban claim credit for Pakistan blast*, CNN.com, Aug. 20, 2008[26] (reporting Taliban claim of responsibility for suicide bombing at Pakistani hospital killing twenty-nine and wounding thirty-five). The Taliban's targets have included soldiers, police officers, political leaders, and civilians in Afghanistan and Pakistan. In the wake of the Taliban's role in assisting al Qaeda and its rising campaign of terror, on July 3, 2002, President Bush added the group to the list of Specially Designated Global Terrorist Groups. *See* Exec. Order No. 13,268, 3 C.F.R. 240 (2002); *see also* Superseding Indictment, *United States v. Khan*, No. 08-cr-00621 (S.D.N.Y. Apr. 21, 2009) (Dkt. No. 14) (alleging defendants provided financial support to Taliban in violation of 21 U.S.C. § 960a).

For years, Afghanistan has been the world's primary source of heroin, accounting for approximately ninety percent of the opium poppy used in the production of heroin. *See* United Nations Office on Drugs and Crime, *Afghanistan Opium Survey 2007*, at iii (October 2007)[27]; *see also* Karen DeYoung, *Afghanistan Opium Crop Sets Record*, Wash. Post, Dec. 2, 2006, at A01[28]; Del Quentin Wilber, *Afghan Farmer Helps Convict Taliban Member in U.S. Court*, Wash. Post, Dec. 23, 2008, at A01.[29] The presence of the Taliban insurgency in the heart of the world's opium poppy fields has sealed an unholy symbiosis among these Islamist extremists and Afghan heroin producers and traffickers. *See* Gov't's Sentencing Mem., *United States v. Mohammed*, No. 06-cr-00357 (D.D.C. Aug. 26, 2008) (Dkt. No. 73) (quoting trial testimony from agent of the U.S. Drug Enforcement Administration ("DEA") that Taliban has taken on a central role in every stage of opium/heroin production and transportation in Afghani-

stan, relies on it as main source of funding, and asserting that the Taliban is involved in over fifty percent of the DEA's Afghanistan heroin cases); *see also id.* (quoting United Nations Office on Drugs and Crime, *Afghanistan Opium Survey 2007*, at iii) ("opium cultivation in Afghanistan is now closely linked to insurgency").[30] In 2006, seeking to give prosecutors a new tool to combat the lethal combination of terrorism and drug trafficking, Congress enacted the narco-terrorism statute, 21 U.S.C. § 960a, which prohibits conduct that would be punishable under the primary federal narcotics statute, 21 U.S.C. § 841(a), if such conduct were committed within the jurisdiction of the United States and if the defendant "know[s] or intend[s] to provide, directly or indirectly, anything of pecuniary value to any person or organization that has engaged or engages in terrorist activity . . . or terrorism[.]" 21 U.S.C. § 960a(a). Section 960a, among other things, is a powerful statute that doubles the minimum punishment that would be imposed on a defendant under the ordinary federal narcotics statute, 21 U.S.C. § 841. *Id.*

In two recent cases, *United States v. Mohammed* and *United States v. Khan*, the government has invoked § 960a to prosecute heroin traffickers aligned with the Taliban.[31] Superseding Indictment, *Mohammed*, No. 06-cr-00357 (D.D.C. Jan. 23, 2008) (Dkt. No. 18); Superseding Indictment, *Khan*, No. 08-cr-00621 (S.D.N.Y. Apr. 21, 2009) (Dkt. No. 14). The trial of Khan Mohammed was reportedly the first ever under the narco-terrorism statute and, according to the government, is believed to be the first trial of a Taliban member in a U.S. court. *See* Gov't's Sentencing Mem. at 2, *Mohammed* (D.D.C. Aug. 26, 2008) (Dkt. No. 73). The case was the product of a well-executed investigation by the DEA. The investigation began when an Afghan farmer, who later testified under the pseudonym "Jaweed," was summoned by a Taliban leader and instructed to find Mohammed and assist him in obtaining rockets to attack a U.S. air base in Jalalabad, not far from Jaweed's village. Wilber, *Afghan Farmer Helps*

Convict Taliban Member in U.S. Court. Jaweed, who did not want to participate in the violence, instead secretly approached an Afghan police chief who in turn introduced him to a DEA agent at the air base. *Id.*; *see also* Gov't's Sentencing Mem. at 4, *Mohammed* (D.D.C. Aug. 26, 2008) (Dkt. No. 73). Jaweed agreed to assist the DEA and was equipped with a recording device. Gov't's Sentencing Mem. at 4, *Mohammed* (D.D.C. Aug. 26, 2008) (Dkt. No. 73). Ultimately, Jaweed made numerous audio recordings in which Mohammed admitted to prior acts of terrorism such as "blowing up government vehicles and shooting rockets at the police chief's office" and expounded on his intent to explode bombs and fire missiles at the air base. *Id.* On instructions from the DEA, Jaweed approached Mohammed purportedly to purchase opium for which he and Mohammed would split the profit. *Id.* at 6. The DEA provided Jaweed with "buy money" and then video-recorded the purchase of opium by Mohammed. *Id.* at 7. According to prosecutors, Mohammed was planning to use commissions from drug sales to support the Taliban and their "terrorist activity." Wilber, *Afghan Farmer Helps Convict Taliban Member in U.S. Court.* Mohammed was also recorded expressing his view that sending the heroin to the United States was "jihad" and "may God turn all the infidels to dead corpses," adding "[w]hether it is by opium or by shooting, this is our common goal." *Id.* Mohammed was arrested on October 29, 2006 (after which he was held for more than a year at Bagram Air Base in Afghanistan), *see* Def.'s Sentencing Mem. at 1, *Mohammed* (D.D.C. Sept. 26, 2008) (Dkt. No. 76), convicted at trial on May 15, 2008, *see* Gov't's Sentencing Mem. at 8, *Mohammed* (D.D.C. Aug. 26, 2008) (Dkt. No. 73), and sentenced to life imprisonment on December 22, 2008, *see* Judgment, *Mohammed* (D.D.C. Dec. 23, 2008) (Dkt. No. 84).

Although the case of Haji Juma Khan remains pending, the indictment's allegations describe a massive heroin organization, and the overt acts described in the conspiracy count detail narcotics transactions, terrorist incidents, and payments being made on Khan's behalf to the Taliban. *See* Indictment, *Khan* (S.D.N.Y. Oct. 21, 2008) (Dkt. No. 1). The specificity of the allegations suggests that the government has a well-developed body of evidence and perhaps cooperating witnesses, as was the case in *Mohammed.*

Federal prosecutors and law enforcement agents have generations of experience in carrying out creative and sometimes daring narcotics-trafficking investigations against many of the largest, most dangerous, and most sophisticated narcotics organizations in the world. The prospect of using that well-developed foundation of experience against narco-terrorists is intriguing and suggests that the government may enjoy future successes against heroin traffickers and their Taliban patrons.[32]

IV.
Detention of Individuals Suspected of Involvement with Terrorism

In approaching the problem of how to deal with suspected terrorists, a recurring and difficult question is that of detention. Is the existing legal framework sufficient to ensure that dangerous terrorists are incapacitated so that they cannot wreak havoc and hurt innocent victims? Or is it necessary to create new legal authority to allow the government to carry out long-term "preventive detention" of persons who may never be charged or brought to trial?

In the past year, there has been ongoing debate over proposals to institutionalize a system for preventive detention. Some commentators have argued that existing law is inadequate and that Congress should fill the perceived gap with a new law permitting preventive detention.[33] Others have questioned the premise that such a system is necessary, and have pointed out that many preventive detention proposals lack essential detail.[34] Although reasonable persons can differ on these questions, we discussed in *In Pursuit of Justice* how existing law grants broad authority to the government to detain alleged terrorists and, accordingly, that proponents of preventive detention have not made a convincing case for the advisability, let alone necessity, of dramatic new measures to give the government additional detention powers outside our traditional legal framework. We also noted that proponents of preventive detention often ignore or downplay the substantial negative consequences of their proposals, including

delay, confusion, constitutional vulnerability, and damage to our national ideals and traditions as well as our standing in the world.[35] Too often, the analysis of preventive detention merely looks at the immediate "benefit" of an increased ability to incapacitate and ignores the negative consequences of such a regime, consequences that admittedly are difficult to quantify but that are real and that may well increase the longer-term danger to the United States.

In *In Pursuit of Justice*, we noted that the government has four well-established sources of legal authority that it can invoke, in appropriate circumstances, to detain individuals suspected of involvement in terrorism: (1) it can seek to detain individuals under the Bail Reform Act after criminal charges are filed; (2) it can detain aliens pending their removal from the United States under the immigration laws; (3) it can detain grand jury witnesses under the material witness statute, 18 U.S.C. § 3144, though detention under this statute is subject to close judicial supervision and is generally available only for a limited period of time; and (4) it can detain members of the enemy under the law of war in order to prevent them from attacking U.S. troops. *In Pursuit of Justice*, at 65-75. In the year since *In Pursuit of Justice* was issued, there has been little change in the legal framework applicable to detention under the bail statute, the immigration laws, or the material witness statute. In particular, detention under the bail statute continues to be an important tool for prosecutors.

Detention under the law of war, however, has been the subject of significant litigation and substantial attention in the past year. Although a comprehensive discussion of this subject is beyond the scope of this 2009 Report, we offer a few observations about the developing legal landscape in this area. In short, we believe that in light of recent court decisions, it is becoming increasingly clear that the law of war affords a manageable and credible framework for determining whether adherents of al Qaeda or associated groups can be detained by the military to prevent them from harming the United States. The law of war has a history that dates back over centuries. In the past year, this body of law has continued to develop and adapt to address the novel features of today's struggle against Islamist extremist terrorists.

In *Hamdi v. Rumsfeld*, the Supreme Court held, in the case of a prisoner captured during the international phase of the armed conflict in Afghanistan, that the government may capture and detain enemy combatants under the law of war "to prevent captured individuals from returning to the field of battle and taking up arms once again." 542 U.S. 507, 518 (2004); *see also id.* (detention under the law of war is a "fundamental and accepted . . . incident to war" and may extend "for the duration of the particular conflict in which [a prisoner is] captured"). The purpose of military detention is not to punish the prisoner; it is instead to disable him from returning to the fight. *See* William Winthrop, *Military Law and Precedents* 788 (rev. 2d ed. 1920) ("A prisoner of war is no convict; his imprisonment is a simple war measure[.]"); *In re Territo*, 156 F.2d 142, 145 (9th Cir. 1946) ("The object of capture is to prevent the captured individual from serving the enemy."). For this reason, the duration of military imprisonment is dictated primarily by the length and ongoing nature of the armed conflict, and not necessarily by the severity of the detainee's individual conduct.

In the terrorism context, U.S. courts have determined that the government's military detention authority flows from the Authorization for Use of Military Force, Pub. L. No. 107-40, 115 Stat. 224 (2001) (AUMF), the post-9/11 congressional resolution that authorized the Executive Branch to "use all necessary and appropriate force against those nations, organizations, or persons" associated with the 9/11 attacks. *Id.* at § 2(a).[36] In *Hamdi*, the Supreme Court held that the AUMF authorizes law-of-war detention of "individuals who fought against the United States in Afghanistan as part of the Taliban" because that organization is "known to have supported the al Qaeda terrorist network responsible for [the September 11] attacks" and thus was targeted by Congress when it enacted the AUMF. 542 U.S. at 518. At the same time, however, the Court recognized that the boundaries of the government's law-of-war detention authority are somewhat uncertain and would have to "be defined by the lower courts as subsequent cases are presented to them." *Id.* at 522 n.1. The question remains, therefore, whether the law of war permits the government to detain individuals who did not actually take up arms against U.S. forces in an international armed conflict or who were captured far away from any combat zone. More pointedly, can the government invoke the law of war to detain, for example, a participant in an al Qaeda supply chain apprehended in Malaysia, or a financier arrested in London, or a sleeper cell agent caught in Virginia?

For a time, it appeared that the Supreme Court might provide further guidance on these questions in the case of *al-Marri v. Pucciarelli*. 129 S. Ct. 680 (2008). In *al-Marri*, which was analyzed extensively in *In Pursuit of Justice* and is discussed above, a Qatari citizen lawfully present in the United States was arrested by the FBI in 2001 in Peoria, Illinois and was held without bail on criminal fraud charges. *Al-Marri v. Wright*, 487 F.3d 160, 164 (4th Cir. 2007). In 2003, shortly before trial, the government abruptly dismissed al-Marri's criminal case with prejudice, designated him as an "enemy combatant," and transferred him to the Consolidated Naval Brig in Charleston, South Carolina, where it held him for years without charge under the law of war. *Id.* at 164-65. After extensive habeas corpus litigation in the lower courts, the en banc Fourth Circuit held, in fractured opinions, that al-Marri could lawfully be held under the law of war—even though he was arrested by the FBI half a world away from the battlefield of Afghanistan—but that he had not been accorded sufficient process to challenge the designation. *See al-Marri v. Pucciarelli*, 534 F.3d 213, 216 (4th Cir. 2008).

In late 2008, the Supreme Court granted certiorari to determine whether the AUMF authorizes, and if so whether the Constitution allows, the detention of a lawful resident alien as an enemy combatant. *See al-Marri*, 129 S. Ct. 680 (granting certiorari). However, in early 2009, while the case was pending before the Supreme Court, the Obama administration indicted al-Marri on criminal charges that he conspired to provide and provided material support for terrorist organizations under 18 U.S.C. § 2339B. Indictment, *United States v. al-Marri*, No. 09-cr-10030 (C.D. Ill. Feb. 26, 2009) (Dkt. No. 3). The government transferred al-Marri out of the Naval Brig and returned him to the criminal justice system in Illinois. Carrie Johnson, *Terrorism Suspect Headed to U.S. Court*, Wash. Post, Feb. 28, 2009, at A2.[37] Two months after being indicted, al-Marri entered a guilty plea to the first count of the indictment and is currently awaiting sentencing. Plea Agreement, *al-Marri* (C.D. Ill. Apr. 30, 2009) (Dkt. No. 22). By transferring al-Marri back to the criminal justice system, the government effectively mooted the Supreme Court litigation. The Supreme Court, in turn, vacated the Fourth Circuit's decision, stripping the lower court ruling of precedential value. *See al-Marri v. Spagone*, 129 S. Ct. 1545 (2009) (granting application to move al-Marri from military custody to criminal justice system and instructing Fourth Circuit to dismiss appeal as moot).[38] Thus, despite the years of litigation in *al-Marri*, the contours of law-of-war detention are still largely undefined by the Supreme

Court, though with the passage of time, the issue has continued to percolate in the lower courts.

The principal catalyst for this lower-court percolation has been *Boumediene v. Bush*, the landmark decision in which the Supreme Court held that Guantánamo detainees are entitled to challenge their detention through habeas corpus litigation in the federal district court in Washington, D.C.[39] 128 S. Ct. 2229 (2008). In the wake of *Boumediene*, scores of prisoners have argued in habeas litigation that they are being unlawfully detained at Guantánamo. The government, in response, has invoked the law of war as the basis for detaining many of the Guantánamo prisoners. All of this has caused the federal district court in Washington, D.C. to focus closely on the boundaries of the government's law-of-war detention authority.

In an early post-*Boumediene* decision rendered shortly before the 2008 presidential election, Judge Richard J. Leon adopted the standard for law-of-war detention that had been offered by the Bush Administration in 2004:

> An 'enemy combatant' is an individual who was part of or supporting Taliban or al Qaeda forces, or associated forces that are engaged in hostilities against the United States or its coalition partners. This includes any person who has committed a belligerent act or has directly supported hostilities in aid of enemy armed forces.

Boumediene v. Bush, 583 F. Supp. 2d 133, 135 (D.D.C. 2008). This expansive language would seemingly authorize the military detention of a broad range of individuals who were "supporting" al Qaeda anywhere in the world.

In January 2009, shortly after President Obama's inauguration, the Department of Justice asked for a stay of proceedings in the Guantánamo litigation so that it could reassess its position on the government's law-of-war detention authority. *See Gherebi v. Obama*, 609 F. Supp. 2d 43, 52-53 (D.D.C. 2009). On March 13, 2009, at the request of several judges in the D.C.

district court, the government offered a slightly revised statement of its authority to detain individuals under the law of war:

> The President has the authority to detain persons that the President determines planned, authorized, committed, or aided the terrorist attacks that occurred on September 11, 2001, and persons who harbored those responsible for those attacks. The President also has the authority to detain persons who were part of, or substantially supported, Taliban or al-Qaida forces or associated forces that are engaged in hostilities against the United States or its coalition partners, including any person who has committed a belligerent act, or has directly supported hostilities, in aid of such enemy armed forces.

Resp'ts' Mem. Regarding the Gov't's Detention Authority Relative to Detainees Held at Guantánamo Bay at 2, *In re Guantánamo Bay Detainee Litig.*, No. 08-mc-00442 (D.D.C. Mar. 13, 2009) (Dkt. No. 1690). The government argued that detention under this definition is authorized by the AUMF as informed by traditional law-of-war principles. Not surprisingly, a number of detainees took issue with the government's definition. They argued that under the Geneva Conventions, in a "non-international" conflict between a state (i.e., the United States) and a non-state organization such as al Qaeda, the government may only detain those individuals who participate "*actively and directly* in hostilities as part of an organized armed force." *See, e.g.*, Pet'rs' Joint Mem. in Reply to Resp'ts' Mem. of Mar. 13, 2009 at 3-4, *Hamlily v. Obama*, No. 05-cv-00763 (D.D.C. Mar. 27, 2009) (Dkt. No. 189) (citing U.S. Navy Handbook) (emphasis in original).

To date, three D.C. district court judges have ruled on this dispute, and all of them have concluded that the government enjoys broad latitude to detain al Qaeda adherents under the law of war even if they did not actually participate in combat against U.S. troops. In an opinion issued on April 22, 2009, Judge Reggie B. Walton strongly rejected the detainees' arguments under

the Geneva Conventions and affirmed that the United States is engaged in an armed conflict against al Qaeda even though it is an organization rather than a state. *See Gherebi*, 609 F. Supp. 2d at 67 ("The Court therefore rejects the petitioners' argument that the laws of war permit a state to detain only individuals who 'directly participate' in hostilities in non-international armed conflicts."). Judge Walton stated pointedly that the Geneva Conventions are "not a suicide pact" providing a free pass to members of an enemy's organization simply because they did not at that moment engage in combat or violence, *id.*; instead, he affirmed the government's definition of its detention authority under the AUMF, but cautioned that the government may detain only those individuals who are associated with al Qaeda in the same way as a member of enemy armed forces in a traditional international armed conflict between two states. *Id.* at 67-69. In this regard, Judge Walton explained that even though al Qaeda is an organization rather than a state, it has a "'leadership and command structure[], however diffuse,'" that resembles the analogous structures in state armed forces. *Id.* at 68 (quoting Curtis A. Bradley & Jack L. Goldsmith, *Congressional Authorization and the War on Terrorism*, 118 Harv. L. Rev. 2048, 2114-15 (May 2005)). According to Judge Walton, it is essential to focus on this structure when considering whether an individual may be detained under the AUMF. *Id.* at 68-69. Thus, Judge Walton held that only those persons who "receive and execute orders" from al Qaeda's "command structure" may be detained as "members of the enemy's armed forces." *Id.* at 68 (internal quotation marks omitted). "Sympathizers, propagandists, and financiers who have no involvement with this 'command structure,' while perhaps members of the enemy organization in an abstract sense, cannot be considered part of the enemy's 'armed forces' and therefore cannot be detained militarily unless they take a direct part in hostilities." *Id.* at 68-69. At the same time, Judge Walton cautioned that an individual may qualify for detention even if he is not an actual fighter:

an al-Qaeda member tasked with housing, feeding, or transporting al-Qaeda fighters could be detained as part of the enemy armed forces notwithstanding his lack of involvement in the actual fighting itself, but an al-Qaeda doctor or cleric, or the father of an al-Qaeda fighter who shelters his son out of familial loyalty, could not be detained assuming such individuals had no independent role in al-Qaeda's chain of command.

Id. at 69. Although Judge Walton ultimately upheld the government's revised standard for law of war detention, he expressed some discomfort with the concept of "support," which he viewed as a criminal law concept and not one historically inherent in the law of war. *See id.* at 69-70. Nevertheless, Judge Walton held that the "support" standard passed muster so long as it was strictly interpreted to encompass only individuals who "were members of the enemy organization's armed forces, as that term is intended under the laws of war, at the time of their capture." *Id.* at 71.

In a subsequent opinion dated May 19, 2009, Judge John D. Bates agreed with much of Judge Walton's reasoning, including his rejection of the detainees' Geneva Conventions arguments. *See Hamlily v. Obama*, 616 F. Supp. 2d 63, 74 (D.D.C. 2009). However, Judge Bates rejected the concept of "support" as an independent basis for detention under the law of war, and ultimately he pared back the government's detention authority in some respects. *Id.* at 69-70. Judge Bates held that the government may detain individuals who were "part of" the Taliban, al Qaeda, or "associated forces" (which he defined to mean "co-belligerents" under the law of war), regardless of whether those individuals actually participated in hostilities. *Id.*[40] In explaining how to determine whether an individual was "part of" an enemy organization such as al Qaeda, Judge Bates adopted Judge Walton's approach:

The key inquiry . . . is not necessarily whether one self-identifies as a member of the organization (although this could be relevant in some cases), but whether the individual functions or participates within or under the command structure of the organization— *i.e.*, whether he receives and executes orders or directions.

Id. at 75. In contrast to Judge Walton, however, Judge Bates held that the government lacks authority to detain individuals who merely "substantially supported" the Taliban or al Qaeda, or "directly supported hostilities" against U.S. forces. *Id.* at 75-77.[41] At the same time, Judge Bates held that evidence that an individual "substantially supported" al Qaeda could be probative in determining whether the person was "part of" of the organization. *Id.* at 76-77.

On May 21, 2009, Judge Royce K. Lamberth of the federal court in Washington adopted Judge Bates' conclusions and reasoning. *See Mattan v. Obama*, ---F. Supp. 2d ---, No. 09-cv-00745, 2009 WL 1425212, at *1 (D.D.C. May 21, 2009). In his brief opinion, Judge Lamberth agreed with Judge Bates that evidence that a detainee offered "support" to "Taliban, al Qaeda, or associated enemy forces" should be considered "in determining whether a detainee should be considered 'part of' those forces." *Id.* at *2.

As this discussion makes clear, U.S. jurisprudence delimiting contours of the government's detention authority under the law of war is still developing, but the picture has come into focus more sharply within the past year. In his May 21, 2009 speech at the National Archives, President Obama indicated that the administration may suggest a more formalized approach to the detention of dangerous individuals who cannot be prosecuted but who "in effect, remain at war with the United States." Barack Obama, U.S. President, Remarks by the President on National Security (May 21, 2009).[42] As Congress and the Executive Branch approach this complex and difficult problem, we believe they should do so with caution and restraint. Our time-tested common law system is already defining the permissible scope of military detention under existing law, interpreted and adapted to address modern circumstances. It may well be the case that the government's existing military detention authority as interpreted by the district courts—coupled with the established legal authority for detention under criminal and immigration law—offers ample latitude to detain dangerous individuals without the need for wholesale creation of new and untested administrative detention regimes that will almost inevitably cause legal and practical headaches and that could, unless great care is taken, undermine our Nation's deepest values and traditions.

V.
Balancing the Demands of Due Process with the Need to Protect Classified Information

As discussed at some length in *In Pursuit of Justice*, the Classified Information Procedures Act (CIPA) establishes a detailed set of procedures designed to balance the defendant's right to a fair trial with the need to protect sensitive evidence that could endanger national security if disclosed. *See In Pursuit of Justice*, at 81-84. In the past year, courts have continued to apply CIPA in terrorism prosecutions, *see, e.g., United States. v. Kassar*, 582 F. Supp. 2d 498, 499-501 (S.D.N.Y. 2008) (considering defendants' request pursuant to CIPA to use classified information at trial and ruling that classified information lacked any probative value and was inadmissible), and we are not aware of any instances in which CIPA's procedures failed and there was a substantial leak of sensitive information as a result of a terrorism prosecution in federal court.

Since last year, appellate courts have reviewed the application of CIPA in two significant terrorism prosecutions. In *United States v. Abu Ali*, the defendant argued that the district court violated his Sixth Amendment Confrontation Clause rights by refusing to allow Abu Ali himself and one of his trial attorneys, who had not obtained the necessary security clearance, to attend and participate in the closed hearings conducted under CIPA. 528 F.3d 210, 244-45 (4th Cir. 2008). A second attorney, who had obtained the requisite security clearances, attended the hearings and advocated on Abu Ali's behalf. *Id.* at 250-52, 252 n.20. Consistent

with CIPA and the rulings of numerous other courts, the Fourth Circuit had little trouble affirming the district court's decision to exclude Abu Ali and his uncleared counsel from the CIPA proceedings in which the district court considered whether a particular document was relevant and material. *See id.* at 253-54 ("A defendant and his counsel, if lacking in the requisite security clearance, must be excluded from hearings that determine what classified information is material and whether substitutions crafted by the government suffice to provide the defendant adequate means of presenting a defense and obtaining a fair trial."). This ruling seems plainly correct, and had the court held otherwise CIPA's purpose would have been thwarted.

Abu Ali also raised a second, more substantial challenge to the CIPA procedures that were used in his case. He argued that the government had improperly shown the jury unredacted versions of two classified documents that Abu Ali himself had only been permitted to view in a redacted form. *Id.* at 244, 253. The documents were coded communications between Abu Ali and the second-in-command of the al Qaeda cell in Medina, Saudi Arabia. *Id.* at 222, 249-50. Although the government did not seek to withhold the substance of the communications from Abu Ali or his uncleared counsel, it contended that certain identifying and forensic information contained on the documents would, if disclosed, reveal sensitive sources and methods used to collect intelligence. *Id.* at 250-51. Accordingly, the government only provided redacted versions of the documents to the defendant and his uncleared counsel. *Id.* at 253. Despite this, the government requested, and the court allowed, that the unredacted documents be submitted to the jury as evidence, without providing unredacted versions to Abu Ali and his uncleared counsel. *Id.* at 254.[43] On appeal, the Fourth Circuit held that it was improper for the district court to "hide the evidence from the defendant, but give it to the jury." *Id.* at 255. Nevertheless, the court went on to find that the submission of the classified documents to the jury was harmless because the substance of the documents was merely cumulative of Abu Ali's own confessions. *Id.* at 257.

Like the Fourth Circuit, the Second Circuit had little difficulty in upholding the exclusion of the defendant from in camera CIPA proceedings and his preclusion from viewing classified documents. *See In re Terrorist Bombings of U.S. Embassies in E. Africa*, 552 F.3d 93, 115-30 (2d Cir. 2008). In *In re Terrorist Bombings*, one of the convicted defendants argued that his exclusion from CIPA proceedings and the entry of a protective order that limited access to classified information to those who could obtain security clearance violated his constitutional rights to counsel, to cross-examine the witnesses against him, to be present at a crucial stage in his trial, to testify at trial, and to present a defense. *Id.* at 115-20. The Second Circuit rejected these arguments, holding that many of the documents were de-classified, others were not relevant, and for others the government agreed to stipulate to certain facts that would obviate the need for their use at trial. *Id.* at 120-30. In addition, the Second Circuit expressly found that "CIPA authorizes district courts to limit access to classified information to persons with a security clearance as long as the application of this requirement does not deprive the defense of evidence that would be 'useful to counter the government's case or to bolster a defense.'" *Id.* at 122 (internal citation omitted).

In *al-Odah v. United States*, a Guantánamo habeas case, the D.C. Circuit did not, strictly speaking, apply CIPA itself, but the court looked to the standards established under CIPA to determine when detainees are entitled to classified information in the discovery stage of habeas proceedings. 559 F.3d 539, 544-45 (D.C. Cir. 2009). The D.C. Circuit relied on settled law in holding that classified information may be disclosed to cleared defense counsel only if it "is both relevant *and material*—in the sense that it is at least helpful to the petitioner's habeas case." *Id.* at 544 (emphasis in original) (relying on precedents such as *Roviaro v. United States*, 353 U.S. 53 (1957); *United States v. Rezaq*, 134 F.3d 1121 (D.C. Cir. 1998); and *United States v. Yunis*, 867 F.2d 617 (D.C. Cir. 1989)). In the unusual (and unusually tangled) posture of Guantánamo habeas litigation, the D.C. Circuit went on to observe that "materiality" in the habeas context could be satisfied if classified evidence were not "directly exculpatory" but, for example, could cast doubt on the reliability of the affirmative evidence proffered by the government as the grounds for continued detention. *Id.* at 545. The D.C. Circuit did not make any determinations of materiality in *al-Odah*, choosing instead to remand the case so that the district court could undertake its own review of the particular items potentially subject to discovery. *Id.* at 546. One influential commentator has criticized the D.C. Circuit's ruling in *al-Odah* as having "dealt a crushing blow to national defense" because it potentially expands the discovery material that the government will be required to disclose in defending Guantánamo habeas litigation. Andrew C. McCarthy, *The War is Over*, Nat'l Rev., Mar. 10, 2009.[44] The actual impact of *al-Odah*, however, remains to be seen, most importantly because the district court has not yet ruled on whether cleared defense counsel is, in fact, entitled to additional discovery. Furthermore, it must be emphasized that if the district court does allow classified discovery to cleared defense counsel in *al-Odah*, CIPA procedures such as substitution and redaction will undoubtedly be invoked, and those procedures have historically served as an effective means of preventing the release of sensitive information that could jeopardize national security. Finally, *al-Odah* was decided in the unique context of Guantánamo habeas litigation, and its implications for conventional criminal cases are uncertain at best.

VI.
The *Miranda* Requirement in Terrorism Cases

A defendant's post-arrest statements often have significant evidentiary value at trial, and indeed can be the central evidence against the defendant. For more than forty years, law enforcement officers have been required to administer *Miranda* warnings—"You have the right to remain silent" and so forth—at the outset of custodial interrogation in order to ensure that any statements made by the defendant will later be admissible in court.

In the intelligence context, *Miranda* does not prevent intelligence officers from interrogating a prisoner, without warnings, after his arrest or capture. *See In Pursuit of Justice*, at 102 (discussing *United States v. Bin Laden*, 132 F. Supp. 2d 168, 189 (S.D.N.Y. 2001)). However, if the government later decides to prosecute the detainee, statements elicited during custodial interrogation but without *Miranda* warnings may not be admissible. In the past year, this scenario of un-*Mirandized* intelligence interrogations has assumed significance. It has been reported that the government conducted extensive intelligence interrogations of Guantánamo detainees without *Miranda* warnings, and the Obama Administration has reportedly expressed doubts about the admissibility of statements made during these interrogations.[45]

It is difficult to assess this issue because it depends on a careful evaluation of the facts, most of which are not a matter of public record, and because the applicability of *Miranda* in the context of intelligence gathering, as opposed to criminal investigations, is still uncertain. However, a few general observations can be made. On one hand, a straightforward application of *Miranda* could indeed pose an obstacle to the admissibility of a defendant's statements during Guantánamo interrogations, especially if they occurred in controlled circumstances resembling traditional police questioning. However, there is a question as to whether courts would uniformly apply the *Miranda* requirement in the context of intelligence gathering, which may be quite different from the domestic law-enforcement scenario for which the *Miranda* doctrine was created.

In *In Pursuit of Justice*, we discussed a related issue— the applicability of *Miranda* in situations where an enemy fighter is captured on the battlefield. *See In Pursuit of Justice*, at 103-05. We noted that soldiers and sailors do not, and need not, administer *Miranda* warnings to individuals who are captured in combat. We also noted that such detainees rarely face criminal prosecution in a domestic court, meaning that the applicability of *Miranda* to battlefield captures is unlikely to be an issue in many actual cases. *See id.* at 103. However, in the event that the government does seek to use a battlefield detainee's post-capture statements in a civilian criminal prosecution, as was the case with John Walker Lindh, there are substantial questions as to whether *Miranda* would apply at all, or whether an exception based on *New York v. Quarles*, 467 U.S. 649 (1984), would obviate the need to administer the warnings. These issues were briefed in the *Lindh* case but were not decided because of Lindh's decision to plead guilty. If a court were to accept the arguments proffered by the government in *Lindh* in the context of at least some intelligence interrogations, then a detainee's post-arrest statements could potentially be admissible if they were made voluntarily, without regard to whether *Miranda* warnings were issued.

Furthermore, even under an orthodox application of *Miranda* doctrine, it is possible that some Guantánamo detainees' statements could be admissible even if no warnings were given. For example, under *Rhode Island v. Innis* and its progeny, *Miranda* does not bar the admissibility of incriminating statements that are not made in response to police questioning or its functional equivalent. 446 U.S. 291, 300-03 (1980). It has been reported that some of the Guantánamo detainees made incriminating statements at preliminary proceedings before military commissions. Most notably, Khalid Sheikh Mohammed spoke to the tribunal convened on March 10, 2007, to determine whether he was properly designated as an enemy combatant against the United States. At that hearing, he made a statement through his designated personal representative in which he pledged allegiance to Bin Laden and confessed to being involved in the planning of about thirty terrorist attacks, including 9/11 and several other completed acts of terrorism. *See* Tr. of Combatant Status Review Tribunal Hr'g for ISN 10024 at 17-19 (Mar. 10, 2007). In a portion of the statement that Khalid Sheikh Mohammed personally delivered to the Tribunal, he referred to himself as a "jackal[] fighting in the night[]" in the "war against America" and an "enemy combatant." *Id.* at 21-22. Such statements could potentially be admissible without regard to *Miranda* because they were not made in response to questioning by interrogators.[46]

In addition, the government might be able to "cleanse" the taint of prior un-*Mirandized* statements by commencing new questioning with proper warnings. A line of cases, including *Oregon v. Elstad* and *Missouri v. Seibert*, holds that failure to provide a *Miranda* warning

in advance of an incriminating statement does not necessarily invalidate a later statement given after a *Miranda* warning was properly administered, especially if the two rounds of interrogation are separated by time and place, are carried out by different interrogators, and are not continuous or overlapping. *See Elstad*, 470 U.S. 298, 314 (1985); *Seibert*, 542 U.S. 600, 615 (2004).[47]

In the future, the government could avoid, or at least substantially reduce, the risk of inadmissible confessions in intelligence interrogations by incorporating a prophylactic *Miranda*-type warning at the outset of questioning. If the detainee waived *Miranda* rights, then his statements would likely be admissible; if not, then the intelligence interrogation could proceed but the defendants' statements would potentially be inadmissible. Intelligence officers might object to the introduction of a law enforcement procedure into their norms and practices, and adding such a step would need to be considered carefully given the obvious importance of developing intelligence that is as robust and accurate as possible in the terrorism context.[48] However, years of experience and empirical data show that the vast majority of arrested defendants waive their *Miranda* rights.[49] This research suggests that it may be worth considering whether to incorporate some form of *Miranda* warnings into intelligence interrogations from which criminal prosecutions may ensue.

More concretely, in the past year the federal appeals courts issued two significant decisions, *Abu Ali* and the *Embassy Bombings* appeal, which clarified the scope of *Miranda* in terrorism cases where defendants were captured and interrogated overseas. We believe both cases will provide effective guidance for prosecutors and agents who seek to conduct overseas interrogations with a view toward ensuring the admissibility of any statements in a federal court.

In *United States v. Abu Ali*, the Fourth Circuit held that *Miranda* warnings are not required when an individual is interrogated by foreign officials unless those officials are acting as agents of or in a "joint venture" with U.S. law enforcement. 528 F.3d 210, 227-28 (4th Cir. 2008). In such situations, the defendant's statements are admissible in a U.S. court as long as they meet the traditional standard of voluntariness. *Id.* at 227. Separately, in the *Embassy Bombings* appeal, the Second Circuit assumed without deciding that some variation of the traditional *Miranda* warning is required when U.S. law enforcement officers interrogate a captured individual overseas and the government later seeks to offer the defendant's statements in court. *In re Terrorist Bombings of U.S. Embassies in E. Africa* (Fifth Amendment Challenges), 552 F.3d 177, 205 (2d Cir. 2008). However, the Second Circuit noted that, even if it were to hold that Miranda governed in these situations, *Miranda* would have to be "applied in a flexible fashion to accommodate the exigencies of local conditions." *Id.* What follows is a more detailed discussion of these two decisions.

A. The *Abu Ali* Case

In *Abu Ali*, the defendant was a United States citizen raised in Northern Virginia who moved to Saudi Arabia at age twenty-one. 528 F.3d at 221. After he arrived in Saudi Arabia, the defendant became affiliated with an al Qaeda cell; planned possible terrorist attacks in the United States, including plots to kill the President; and received training in firearms, explosives, and forgery. *See id.* at 221-24. In 2003, after being arrested by Saudi authorities, the Saudi counterterrorism agency, the Mabahith, interrogated the defendant over the course of a two-week period. *See id.* at 224-25. The interrogations resulted in several written confessions and a videotaped confession. *Id.* at 224. During one day of interrogation, June 15, 2003, the Mabahith asked Abu Ali certain questions that the FBI submitted, and the Mabahith allowed the FBI to observe that interrogation via a one-way mirror. *See id.* at 225. In 2005, Abu Ali was turned over to the United States to

face criminal charges in federal court. *Id.* At the trial, the government presented evidence of the defendant's incriminating statements during his interrogation in Saudi Arabia, and he was convicted and sentenced to thirty years' imprisonment. *Id.* at 225-26. On appeal, the defendant argued that he had not been given *Miranda* warnings and that, as a result, his statements to the Saudi authorities should have been suppressed. *Id.* at 228.

A Fourth Circuit panel rejected the defendant's arguments and held, by a 2-1 vote, that *Miranda* did not apply to the questioning by the Saudi authorities. *Id.* at 227-30. With respect to the interrogation observed by the FBI, the panel majority found that the Saudis were not engaged in a "joint venture" that would trigger *Miranda* because the Saudis "rejected a majority of the questions proposed by the FBI," and U.S. agents were not actually "present in the interrogation room," and therefore the U.S. agents did not "actively participate" in the interrogation. *Id.* at 228-29, 229 n.5. The panel derived the "general rule" that "mere presence at an interrogation does not constitute the 'active' or 'substantial' participation necessary for a 'joint venture,' but coordination and direction of an investigation or interrogation does." *Id.* at 229 (citations omitted). The majority reasoned that to expand the application of *Miranda* to cases where U.S. law enforcement officials were present, but did not actively participate, would stray from *Miranda*'s purpose of regulating the conduct of U.S. law enforcement officers and "could potentially discourage the United States and its allies from cooperating in criminal investigations of an international scope." *Id.* at 229 n.5. The majority emphasized that "[t]o impose all of the particulars of American criminal process upon foreign law enforcement agents goes too far in the direction of dictation, with all its attendant resentments and hostilities." *Id.*[50]

Later in the *Abu Ali* opinion, all three members of the panel affirmed the lower court's ruling, which was based on an exhaustive fourteen-day evidentiary hearing, that the defendant had voluntarily made his post-arrest statements to the Saudi authorities. *Id.* at 232-34. The Fourth Circuit emphasized the testimony of both Saudi and American officials who observed Abu Ali during the period of his interrogation and testified that he "showed no physical or psychological signs of impairment" despite Abu Ali's claims that he was tortured by Saudi authorities. *Id.* The Fourth Circuit's discussion underscores the importance of making accurate contemporaneous observations of a defendant who is being interrogated overseas—including obtaining contemporaneous medical exams if possible—in order to deter or detect any possible improper behavior by foreign law enforcement officers and to rebut fabricated claims of torture that may later be offered by defendants who are seeking to have their post-arrest statements excluded. *See id.* at 232-33 (noting approvingly that the lower court had issued a 113-page opinion in which it expressed doubts about the credibility of Abu Ali's claims of torture and that the lower court had carefully weighed the evidence in this regard).

B. The *Embassy Bombings* Case

The *Embassy Bombings* case presented a different factual scenario in which the overseas interrogation was carried out directly by U.S. law enforcement officials including FBI agents, a New York Police Department detective, and an Assistant United States Attorney (AUSA). 552 F.3d at 181. The questioning occurred over a nine-day period in Kenya in the aftermath of the 1998 bombings of the U.S. embassies in Nairobi, Kenya, and Dar es Salaam, Tanzania. *Id.* at 181-83. The defendant was given a variant of the traditional Miranda warnings on a pre-printed FBI "Advice of Rights" (AOR) form. *Id.* at 181. Although this form advised the defendant that he had the right to remain silent, it did not give any information about a right to counsel, stating only that the defendant would have a right to counsel if he was being interrogated in the United States but that "[b]ecause we are not in the United States, we cannot

ensure that you will have a lawyer appointed for you before any questioning." *Id.* Before trial, the lower court had held that *Miranda* was applicable to the interrogation, even though it occurred halfway around the world, and that the AOR form was defective because it too easily dismissed the availability of counsel. *Id.* at 188-90. The lower court held, however, that oral clarifying remarks by the AUSA were sufficient to cure the deficiencies of the AOR form, that the defendant had knowingly waived his clarified *Miranda* rights, and that the defendant's statements after the AUSA's clarifications were therefore admissible. *Id.* at 190-91.

On appeal, the Second Circuit assumed (but did not expressly decide) that "the *Miranda* 'warning/waiver' framework generally governs the admissibility in our domestic courts of custodial statements obtained by U.S. officials from individuals during their detention under the authority of foreign governments." *Id.* at 203. The Second Circuit held, however, that the lower court had applied *Miranda* too rigidly in rejecting the language of the AOR. *Id.* at 205-09; *see also id.* at 205 ("[W]here *Miranda* has been applied to overseas interrogations by U.S. agents, it has been so applied in a flexible fashion to accommodate the exigencies of local conditions."). Unlike the lower court, the Second Circuit found that the "AOR substantially complied with whatever *Miranda* requirements were applicable," *id.* at 209, noting that it "presented defendants with a factually accurate statement of their right to counsel under the U.S. Constitution" and that "it also explained that the effectuation of that right might be limited by the strictures of criminal procedure in a foreign land," *id.* at 206. Emphasizing that U.S. law enforcement officers working overseas are not required to "study local criminal procedure and urge local officials to provide suspects with counsel," *id.* at 207, the Second Circuit summarized that "*Miranda* requires government agents to be the conduits of information to detained suspects— both as to (1) their rights under the U.S. Constitution to the presence and appointment of counsel at custodial interrogations and (2) the procedures through which they might be able to vindicate those rights under local law. It does not compel the police to serve as advocates for detainees before local authorities, endeavoring to expand the rights and privileges available under local law," *id.* at 208 (emphasis omitted).[51]

VII.
Broad Array of Evidence Successfully Introduced in Terrorism Prosecutions

As with all prosecutions, evidence is the foundation on which any terrorism prosecution is built, and evidence must be legally admissible before it can be considered by a jury. In federal court, the admissibility of evidence is governed by the Federal Rules of Evidence and, in some situations, by the requirements of the Constitution. The events of the past year confirm that, in general, federal evidentiary rules do not preclude prosecutors from introducing reliable, probative evidence in terrorism prosecutions. Again, the *Abu Ali* case is instructive. In that case, the Fourth Circuit provided a road map for how the government can secure testimony from witnesses who are located overseas without violating a defendant's constitutional right to confront the witnesses against him. *Abu Ali*, 528 F.3d 210, 238-43 (4th Cir. 2008). Separately, the Second Circuit reversed a major terrorism-financing conviction in *United States v. al-Moayad* based on a litany of trial errors by the presiding judge. 545 F.3d 139 (2d Cir. 2008). The *al-Moayad* reversal stands as a reminder of the importance of careful attention to evidentiary requirements. Finally, two new terrorism prosecutions, *United States v. Ahmed* and *United States v. al-Delaema*, illustrate the broad array of evidence, including electronic communications, that may be available to the government in particular cases. *See Ahmed*, No. 07-cr-00647 (N.D. Ohio); *al-Delaema*, No. 05-cr-00337 (D.D.C.).

A. *United States v. Abu Ali—* the Confrontation Clause

The Sixth Amendment to the United States Constitution guarantees that in "all criminal prosecutions, the accused shall enjoy the right . . . to be confronted with the witnesses against him." U.S. Const. amend. VI. Traditionally, the Confrontation Clause mandates that the defendant be given "a face-to-face meeting with witnesses appearing before the trier of fact." *Coy v. Iowa*, 487 U.S. 1012, 1016 (1988). In some terrorism cases, however, the witnesses are located far away in foreign countries, which raises the question whether it is possible to reconcile the defendant's right to confront the witnesses against him with the practical difficulties of securing live, in-person testimony from foreign witnesses. In *Abu Ali*, the Fourth Circuit answered this question in the affirmative, endorsing the careful steps taken by the trial judge to ensure that the defendant and his counsel had a fair opportunity to confront adverse witnesses in Saudi Arabia.

The defendant in *Abu Ali*, a native of Virginia, moved at age twenty-one to Saudi Arabia, where he became affiliated with an al Qaeda cell and planned serious terrorism attacks in the United States. 528 F.3d at 221-24. On June 8, 2003, a little over a month after deadly al Qaeda bombings in Riyadh, the Mabahith, Saudi

Arabia's anti-terrorism law enforcement agency, arrested Abu Ali in Saudi Arabia and held him in custody there. *Id.* at 224. Abu Ali eventually gave incriminating written and videotaped confessions to the Saudi authorities. *Id.* at 238. He was subsequently turned over to the United States to face terrorism charges in federal court in Virginia. *Id.* at 225. Before trial, Abu Ali moved to suppress his confessions, arguing that he had been tortured by the Mabahith, and that his confessions were therefore inadmissible. *Id.* at 225-26, 232.

In order to assess Abu Ali's claims of torture, it was necessary for the trial court to hear testimony from the Mabahith officers who had interrogated Abu Ali. Also, in order to admit the confessions at trial, it was important for the Mabahith officers to explain to the jury the circumstances under which the confession had been obtained. All of this presented a logistical conundrum, however, because the Saudi government did not permit the Mabahith officers to travel to the United States, and they could not be compelled to travel because they fell outside the subpoena power of a U.S. court. *Id.* at 239. The Saudi government allowed the Mabahith officers to participate in a pre-trial deposition held in Saudi Arabia, which could be videotaped and played before the jury at trial under Rule 15 of the Federal Rules of Criminal Procedure, but this procedure would not allow Abu Ali to have a face-to-face encounter with the witnesses unless he could somehow be transported back to Saudi Arabia for the depositions—a scenario that could not be arranged because of security considerations. *Id.*

Attempting to resolve this logistical dilemma, the district court devised an elaborate solution under which the prosecutors, a translator, and two defense attorneys attended the depositions in Saudi Arabia while a third defense attorney sat with Abu Ali in a courtroom in Virginia. *Id.*

> A live, two-way video link was used to transmit the proceedings to a courtroom in Alexandria. This permitted Abu Ali and one of his attorneys to see and hear the testimony contemporaneously; it also al-lowed the Mabahith officers to see and hear Abu Ali as they testified. . . . [B]oth the witnesses and Abu Ali were videotaped during the depositions, so that the jury could [later] see their reactions.

Id. at 239-40. The judge was present in the courtroom with Abu Ali in Virginia to rule on evidentiary objections, and Abu Ali had a cell phone link with his attorneys in Saudi Arabia to permit private conferences during breaks. *Id.* at 240. With these arrangements in place, the trial judge presided over seven days of testimony, in which the Mabahith officers testified extensively and were subject to full cross-examination about all aspects of Abu Ali's treatment by the Saudi authorities, including the events leading up to his confessions. *Id.* At trial, relevant portions of the deposition videotape were played for the jury. *Id.* at 241-42.

On appeal, the Fourth Circuit upheld these procedures under the Confrontation Clause. Noting the strong preference for in-person confrontation rights, the Fourth Circuit nevertheless relied on Supreme Court precedent holding that testimony may be received without in-person confrontation if: (a) "the denial of 'face-to-face confrontation' [is] 'necessary to further an important public policy,'" and (b) "the district court . . . ensure[s] that protections are put in place so that 'the reliability of the testimony is otherwise assured.'" *Id.* at 240 (quoting *Maryland v. Craig*, 497 U.S. 836, 850 (1990)). In *Abu Ali*, the Fourth Circuit found that both of these conditions were satisfied. *Id.*

First, the Fourth Circuit found that "[t]he prosecution of those bent on inflicting mass civilian casualties or assassinating high public officials is . . . just the kind of important public interest contemplated by" the Supreme Court's decision in *Maryland v. Craig. Id.* at 241. The court held that insisting on in-person confrontation in all circumstances would "in some circumstances limit the ability of the United States to further its fundamental interest in preventing terrorist attacks." *Id.* The court added:

It is unquestionable that the struggle against terrorism is one of global dimension and that the United States depends upon its allies for logistical support and intelligence in this endeavor. This cooperation can result in foreign officials possessing information vital to prosecutions occurring in American courts. If the government is flatly prohibited from deposing foreign officials anywhere but in the United States, this would jeopardize the government's ability to prosecute terrorists using the domestic criminal justice system.

Id.

Turning to the other prong of the *Maryland v. Craig* test, the Fourth Circuit held that the procedures devised by the trial court were sufficiently robust to assure the reliability of the deposition testimony, thus permitting the videotape to be shown to the jury. *Id.* at 241-42. Accordingly, the Fourth Circuit upheld the admissibility of the videotaped testimony. Going forward, it is likely that prosecutors and courts will look to *Abu Ali* as a template for how to secure testimony from foreign witnesses in important terrorism cases.[52]

B. *United States v. al-Moayad*—the importance of attention to evidentiary requirements

The government suffered a setback in *al-Moayad*, in which the Second Circuit threw out a major terrorism-financing conviction and remanded for a new trial based on a series of trial errors by the presiding judge. In *al-Moayad*, the lead defendant, a Yemeni cleric, was arrested in Germany along with a co-defendant after an undercover FBI investigation featuring a controversial informant whose strange behavior became a focus of the trial. 545 F.3d at 145-50. The informant, Mohammed al-Anssi, had approached the FBI soon after 9/11 and offered to assist in an investigation of al-Moayad, who al-Anssi stated was involved in supplying money, arms, and recruits to terrorist groups. *Id.* at 145-46. The

FBI sent al-Anssi on three separate trips to Yemen, where he met with al-Moayad and ultimately proposed a sting operation under which al-Moayad would travel to Frankfurt, Germany to meet with a "donor" (in reality, another FBI informant) who was purportedly interested in donating millions of dollars to support terrorism. *See id.* at 146-48. The meeting in Germany was secretly recorded by the government, and al-Moayad and a co-defendant were arrested shortly after the meeting ended. *See id.* at 150.

At trial, the defense argued that al-Moayad ran legitimate charitable organizations and that the government had entrapped him into meeting with the informants. *Id.* at 153-54. In support of this theory, the defense pointed to many of the taped conversations from the meetings in Germany where al-Moayad seemingly resisted discussing terrorist activities and instead emphasized purportedly legitimate charitable activities. *See id.* at 148-50. In a bold tactical move, the defense also called al-Anssi as a witness in the defense case. *See id.* at 154-55. (The government had chosen not to call al-Anssi as a witness during its case-in-chief despite his central role in the investigation. *See id.* at 145-46.)

In his testimony, al-Anssi admitted that the FBI paid him $100,000 but that he sought millions of dollars more and that, in a bid to get more money from the FBI, he set himself on fire in front of the White House. *See id.* at 146, 154. Al-Anssi also admitted that he had a prior felony conviction for writing bad checks. *See id.* at 154. Seeking to further undermine al-Anssi's testimony, defense counsel emphasized that al-Anssi had not recorded any of his meetings with al-Moayad in Yemen and repeatedly asked al-Anssi questions suggesting that there was no "recording or . . . piece of paper that's prior to Frankfurt" demonstrating that al-Moayad had funneled money for jihad. *Id.*; *see also id.* at 155 ("'I ask you before you went to Frankfurt, was there anything, any document or any recording supporting what you've told this jury today?'"). On cross-examination, in an effort to rehabilitate al-Anssi's credibility, the government offered incriminating notes that al-Anssi had taken during his unrecorded meetings with al-Moayad in Yemen. *Id.* at 155. The trial court admitted the notes as substantive evidence, despite their quality as hearsay, and the government argued from the notes extensively in its summation. *See id.* at 155, 170.

In its rebuttal case, the government also offered an unrelated piece of documentary evidence—an "application for a mujahidin training camp" that had been filled out in 1999 by an unknown individual named "Abu Jihad" who had listed al-Moayad as a reference on the form. *See id.* at 156. The government did not offer evidence about the identity or background of Abu Jihad; it merely offered the form at trial to show al-Moayad's connection to terrorism. *See id.* The government also offered the testimony of a cooperating defendant named Yahya Goba, an American citizen who had attended an al Qaeda training camp in 2001 and who had filled out a similar form. *See id.* Goba did not have any dealings with al-Moayad or "Abu Jihad," but he nevertheless was permitted to offer extensive testimony about his experience in a training camp in Afghanistan, including two visits to the camp by Osama bin Laden. *See id.* at 156-57.

The jury convicted al-Moayad and his co-defendant, and the trial judge sentenced them to extensive terms of imprisonment. *Id.* at 158-59. On appeal, however, the Second Circuit threw out the convictions, highlighting various pieces of evidence that had been improperly admitted. *See id.* at 159-79. In particular, the Second Circuit found that the trial court had allowed the government to elicit improperly wide-ranging testimony from Goba, whose inflammatory testimony about his experience in an al Qaeda training camp was, according to the Second Circuit, unfairly prejudicial to al-Moayad. *See id.* at 162-63.[53] The Second Circuit also criticized the trial judge for admitting al-Anssi's notes as substantive evidence given their status as hearsay, though the Second Circuit suggested that the notes could poten-

tially have been admitted for a more limited purpose if a proper jury instruction had been given. *See id.* at 166-69. Finally, although the Second Circuit held that the mujahidin form had been properly authenticated despite the less-than-perfect chain of custody, *see id.* at 172-73 (quoting *United States v. Gagliardi*, 506 F.3d 140, 151 (2d Cir. 2007) (noting that "'the bar for authentication of evidence is not particularly high,' and proof of authentication may be direct or circumstantial"), the court noted that the form was hearsay and that the government had not met the necessary requirements for admissibility as a co-conspirator statement, *see id.* at 172-74.

Although the reversal in *al-Moayad* was a significant blow for the government, analysis of the Second Circuit's opinion reveals that most of the trial court's errors were garden-variety trial mistakes that do not suggest any systemic or structural flaw particular to terrorism prosecutions. Further, had the trial court made a more careful record of its evidentiary rulings, and had the court more diligently required the use of limiting instructions and proper evidentiary foundations, it is probable that at least some of the disputed evidence could have been properly admitted. Therefore, we do not believe the *al-Moayad* reversal reveals any particular weakness in the overall ability of the federal courts to handle terrorism cases. Nevertheless, the Second Circuit's decision is a strong reminder of the importance of adhering to the Federal Rules of Evidence, even in important and high-profile terrorism cases.

C. *United States v. Ahmed* and *United States v. al-Delaema*— illustrating the breadth of available evidence in terrorism cases

In the past year, the government secured guilty pleas in two terrorism prosecutions that were filed, respectively, in Toledo and Washington, D.C. *See* Plea Agreement as to Zubair Ahmed, *Ahmed* (N.D. Ohio Jan. 15, 2009)

(Dkt. No. 131); Plea Agreement as to Khaleel Ahmed, *Ahmed* (N.D. Ohio Jan. 15, 2009) (Dkt. No. 132); Plea Agreement, *al-Delaema* (D.D.C. Feb. 26, 2009) (Dkt. No. 92). Although these cases are unrelated, they illustrate the tremendous breadth of evidence that is potentially available to the government in prosecuting alleged terrorists. In particular, both the *Ahmed* and *al-Delaema* cases exemplify the government's successful use of electronic evidence to build strong terrorism cases.

In *Ahmed*, two Chicago cousins, Zubair Ahmed and Khaleel Ahmed, each pled guilty to one count of conspiracy to provide material support to terrorists in violation of 18 U.S.C. § 2339A. Superseding Information, *Ahmed* (N.D. Ohio Jan. 15, 2009) (Dkt. No. 129); *see also* Press Release, U.S. Dep't of Justice, Chicago Cousins Plead Guilty to Conspiracy to Provide Material Support to Terrorists (Jan. 15, 2009).[54] The theory of the prosecution was that the cousins had conspired, over a period of almost three years, to provide themselves as "personnel" to perform violent acts against U.S. military forces in Iraq or Afghanistan. Superseding Information, *Ahmed* (N.D. Ohio Jan. 15, 2009) (Dkt. No. 129). In its original indictment, the government laid out in detail the evidence of the cousins' plot. *See* Indictment, *Ahmed* (N.D. Ohio Dec. 13, 2007) (Dkt. No. 1). The indictment contains an impressive array of evidence that is as noteworthy for its variety as for its probative force. Among other things, it describes the following types of evidence against the Ahmed cousins:

- Travel records showing that the cousins traveled together to Egypt in 2004, *id.* ¶¶ 15-17;

- Intercepted emails in which Zubair Ahmed wrote to another individual about "the need to prepare for 'the final war of Islam'" and plans to reach "the 'third' level, their code word for active participation in violent jihad," and in which the two men discussed overcoming their family members' objections to violent jihad, *id.* ¶¶ 22-23, 31;

- Testimony of a cooperating witness with a military background who agreed to provide the cousins with "weapons, tactical, and other military-style training," *id.* ¶¶ 18-19;

- Intercepted telephone conversations in which Zubair Ahmed spoke to another person about the plan to engage in violent jihad, and in which Zubair and Khaleel Ahmed discussed cleaning computer files to delete references to the 2004 Egypt trip and obtaining particular types of firearms in Illinois, *id.* ¶¶ 34-42;

- False statements to federal agents who interviewed both cousins, *id.* ¶¶ 43-45; and

- Records of Zubair Ahmed's purchase of a firearm in Illinois and the cousins' purchase of ammunition at a different location, *id.* ¶¶ 46-47.

Taken as a whole, this body of evidence exemplifies the many ways the government can prove its case, from cooperating witnesses to traditional business records and travel records to intercepted telephone calls and emails.

Al-Delaema was the first case in which U.S. courts were used to prosecute an individual for terrorism against U.S. troops in Iraq. *See* Gov't's Sentencing Mem. at 1, *al-Delaema* (D.D.C. Apr. 3, 2009) (Dkt. No. 99). The defendant, Wesam al-Delaema, was a native of Iraq who settled in the Netherlands in 1993, became a Dutch citizen in 2001, and worked in the Netherlands as a hairdresser and in an auto repair shop. *Id.* at 5. In 2003, al-Delaema became outraged when U.S. forces invaded Iraq. *See id.* at 5-6. In October 2003, he and a friend drove their cars from the Netherlands to Iraq, videotaping much of the trip, and al-Delaema then proceeded to videotape himself meeting in Iraq with masked figures at night outside Fallujah as the group planted improvised explosive devices (IEDs) in the roadway in an effort to kill U.S. troops. *See id.* at 7-14. The videotapes were remarkably comprehensive and incriminating; they depicted al-Delaema and others making impassioned speeches in which they described their plan to mine the roadway in explicit detail. *See id.* at 11-14. For example, the videotape depicts al-Delaema himself saying:

> We, the Mujahideen of Fallujah, have a plan, God willing, for today. With God's help, and if the Americans enter, we will hit them with timed mine, by way of remote. . . . Controlled by remote from afar. God willing, if the hit is successful, we will hunt them. . . . We will show you, in a short while, the site where we hide the mines and how the operation is conducted.

Id. at 10. The government was able to document the time and location where the videotapes were filmed by comparing the images in the video to known aerial photographs of the Fallujah area as well as tables showing the position of the sun at various longitudes and latitudes at various times of the year. *See id.* at 15. The government's analysis of the Fallujah video also matched up with locations of known IED attacks in the month of October 2003. *Id.*

After al-Delaema returned to the Netherlands, the Dutch police imposed a court-ordered wiretap on his phone. *See id.* at 16. On the wiretap, the Dutch authorities intercepted conversations in which al-Delaema spoke with others about martyrdom, war, insurgent attacks in Iraq, and obtaining video recordings of attacks. *See id.* at 16-17. In one intercepted call, al-Delaema offered to obtain a video camera for a colleague to take to Iraq to use in filming attacks against Americans. *See id.* at 17. Later, after he had been extradited to the United States, al-Delaema challenged the admissibility of the Dutch wiretap evidence, but the district judge ruled that the wiretaps had been lawfully conducted under Dutch law after holding a week-long evidentiary hearing for which Dutch law enforcement agents traveled to Washington, D.C. to give testimony. *See id.* at 2-4.

At the time of al-Delaema's arrest in the Netherlands, the Dutch authorities seized numerous incriminating videos from his residence, including the October 2003 video of the IED operation outside Fallujah. *See id.* at 19. Also, al-Delaema made numerous, videotaped false exculpatory statements when the Dutch police asked him about his activities in Iraq. *See id.* at 21-29.

In January 2007, after losing an extradition battle, al-Delaema was transported to Washington, D.C. to face federal terrorism charges. *See id.* at 2. On February 26, 2009, after extensive pre-trial motion practice, al-Delaema pled guilty to one count of conspiracy to murder U.S. nationals abroad in violation of 18 U.S.C. § 2332(b)(2).[55] *See* Plea Agreement at 2, *al-Delaema* (D.D.C. Feb. 26, 2009) (Dkt. No. 92). He stipulated to a twenty-five-year prison sentence which will be served in the Netherlands. *See id.* at 2, 4-5. Assessing the case, it is clear that the success of the prosecution rests in large part on the varied and vivid electronic and videotaped evidence that was available for use against the defendant.

VIII.
Recent Developments in Sentencing Terrorism Defendants

In the past year, courts have continued to impose severe sentences on defendants convicted of terrorism-related offenses, whether by trial or guilty plea. Much of the litigation has focused on the special provision of the Sentencing Guidelines, § 3A1.4, which provides for dramatically increased sentencing exposure for defendants who are convicted of a crime that "involved, or was intended to promote, a federal crime of terrorism." U.S.S.G. § 3A1.4. In most cases, this provision would automatically trigger a Guidelines range of no less than 210-262 months.

Since *In Pursuit of Justice* was released, courts have continued to apply the terrorism sentencing enhancement under § 3A1.4. The Fourth Circuit addressed the application of the terrorism enhancement in two recent cases. *See United States v. Benkahla*, 530 F.3d 300 (4th Cir. 2008); *United States v. Chandia*, 514 F.3d 365 (4th Cir. 2008). In *Benkahla*, the court affirmed the district court's application of the terrorism enhancement against a defendant who was convicted of making false statements to the FBI and obstructing justice in a terrorism investigation after being acquitted on underlying terrorism charges. 530 F.3d at 311-13. In *Chandia*, the Fourth Circuit vacated the defendant's 180-month sentence and remanded for resentencing on the grounds that the district court appeared to have incorrectly determined that the terrorism enhancement automatically applied to a conviction under the material

support statute. *See* 514 F.3d at 375-76. The court remanded for a determination of whether the defendant had the intent required for the enhancement to be applicable. *Id.* at 376.

Several courts have found that application of the terrorism enhancement does not require "transnational conduct." In *United States v. Salim*, the defendant attacked a corrections officer in New York City while awaiting trial on charges related to the 1998 Embassy Bombings in East Africa. 549 F.3d 67, 70 (2d Cir. 2008). The facts showed that the attack was in retaliation for the court's refusal to allow a substitution of counsel in the underlying case. *See id.* at 70-71. The trial court had declined to include the terrorism enhancement in its calculation of the applicable Guidelines range on the grounds that the defendant did not engage in a "federal crime of terrorism" because his conduct in attacking the guard was not "conduct transcending national boundaries" under § 2332b(a)(1). *Id.* at 72.

On the government's cross-appeal, the Second Circuit found that application of the terrorism enhancement does not require "transnational conduct." *See id.* at 76-79. The court held that:

> The sentencing enhancement for a federal crime of terrorism is not limited to conduct that constitutes an offense under section 2332b; it applies to any con-

duct that meets the definition of subsection (g)(5). Congress could have defined 'Federal crime of terrorism' to include a requirement that the offense conduct transcend national boundaries, but it did not. Instead, it defined two distinct terms, 'Federal crime of terrorism' and 'conduct transcending national boundaries,' and neither term references the other.

Id. at 78. The court concluded that the sentence was unreasonable based on the procedural failure to calculate the appropriate Guidelines range, and remanded to the district court for resentencing. *See id.* at 79. In a separate case, the Eleventh Circuit agreed with this analysis. *See United States v. Garey*, 546 F.3d 1359, 1361-63 (11th Cir. 2008) (rejecting requirement of "transnational conduct" for application of the terrorism enhancement).

In *United States v. Abu Ali*, perhaps the most interesting terrorism-related sentencing decision of the past year because of the breadth of issues it covers, the Fourth Circuit found that the district court abused its discretion in deviating downward from the applicable Guidelines range. *See* 528 F.3d 210, 258-65 (4th Cir. 2008). The dissent suggested that, in so doing, the Fourth Circuit created a standard of review for terrorism sentences that is less deferential than the ordinary abuse-of-discretion standard. *See id.* at 270-72 (Motz, J., dissenting).

As outlined above, Abu Ali was convicted of serious crimes including material support, conspiracy to assassinate the President, and conspiracy to destroy aircraft. *See id.* at 225-26. Although Abu Ali was subject to a life sentence under the Guidelines, the district court deviated downward, sentencing him to 360 months imprisonment. *See id.* at 258-59. In reaching that sentence, the district court compared Abu Ali's case with the *Lindh* case—in which a U.S. citizen received a twenty-year sentence after being captured in Afghanistan fighting alongside the Taliban against U.S. forces—along with the Oklahoma City bombing prosecutions of

Timothy McVeigh and Terry Nichols. *See id.* at 259. The trial court found that Abu Ali's case was similar to the *Lindh* case and distinguishable from *McVeigh* and *Nichols*. *See id.* As a result, the court reasoned, under 18 U.S.C. § 3553(a)(6), the need to avoid unwarranted sentence disparities merited a downward adjustment from the Guidelines range. *See id.*

On appeal, the Fourth Circuit vacated Abu Ali's sentence and remanded for resentencing on the grounds that the forty percent reduction imposed by the trial court was not reasonable. *See id.* at 261-65. The court held that the *Lindh* case was not comparable based on a number of factors, including that Lindh pled guilty, expressed remorse, and never intended to fight against the United States. *See id.* at 262-64. Conversely, the court held that the *McVeigh* and *Nichols* cases should not have been distinguished on the ground that Abu Ali's plans were thwarted, because Abu Ali had taken significant steps and the offense "clearly contemplates incomplete conduct." *Id.* at 264. In dissent, Judge Motz argued that the *Abu Ali* majority in effect created a less deferential standard apparently applicable only for terrorism cases, *see id.* at 271 (Motz, J., dissenting); the majority disagreed, insisting that it had merely applied settled sentencing law in light of the "immensity and scale of wanton harm that was and remains Abu Ali's plain and clear intention," *id.* at 269.

Finally, the recent case of *United States v. al-Delaema* illustrates the complications that may arise in extraditing and trying foreign citizens for terrorism crimes under the laws of the United States, given the tendency of the U.S. system to dole out harsh sentences for such violations. As outlined above, al-Delaema, a native of Iraq who became a Dutch citizen in 2001, traveled from his home in the Netherlands to Iraq, where he helped bury improvised explosive devices (IEDs) in and around Fallujah with the intent that the IEDs would explode and destroy American vehicles, killing Americans riding inside. *See* Statement of Offense, *United States v. al-Delaema*, No. 05-cr-00337 (D.D.C. Feb. 26, 2009)

(Dkt. No. 93); Gov't's Sentencing Mem. at 5-15, *al-Delaema* (D.D.C. Apr. 3, 2009) (Dkt. No. 99). Al-Delaema was indicted in the District of Columbia in September 2005, and fought vigorously against extradition to the United States, arguing that he would not be treated fairly and humanely in the U.S. criminal justice system. *See* Indictment, *al-Delaema* (D.D.C. Sept. 9, 2005) (Dkt. No. 5); Gov't's Sentencing Mem. at 1-2, *al-Delaema* (D.D.C. Apr. 3, 2009) (Dkt. No. 99). Al-Delaema was extradited in January 2007, and as in other extraditions between the United States and the Netherlands, the United States agreed that, upon the defendant's conviction and sentencing, the United States would not oppose any request by the defendant to serve his sentence in the Netherlands. *See* Gov't's Sentencing Mem. at 1, *al-Delaema* (D.D.C. Apr. 3, 2009) (Dkt. No. 99); Plea Agreement at 4-5, *al-Delaema* (D.D.C. Feb. 26, 2009) (Dkt. No. 92).

Al-Delaema subsequently pled guilty to one count of conspiracy to kill a national of the United States outside the United States in violation of 18 U.S.C. § 2332(b). *See* Judgment, *al-Delaema* (D.D.C. Apr. 17, 2009) (Dkt. No. 109). Pursuant to the plea agreement, the parties agreed that a sentence of twenty-five years was appropriate. *See* Plea Agreement at 2, *al-Delaema* (D.D.C. Feb. 26, 2009) (Dkt. No. 92). The plea agreement also stated that the United States agreed not to oppose defendant's request to serve his sentence in the Netherlands, should he request it, and that all parties understood that the defendant would be re-sentenced by a judge in the Netherlands upon his return to that country. *See id.* at 4-5. On April 16, 2009, al-Delaema was sentenced to twenty-five years in accordance with the plea agreement. *See* Minute Entry, *al-Delaema* (D.D.C. Apr. 16, 2009); Judgment, *al-Delaema* (D.D.C. Apr. 17, 2009) (Dkt. No. 109).

Al-Delaema will likely be transported to the Netherlands in the coming months and the issue of his sentence be revisited by a Dutch court. Al-Delaema's attorney has stated that he is confident that al-Delaema will receive a reduced sentence in the Netherlands because the sentencing rules there are not as severe as in the United States. *See* Nedra Pickler, *Judge Urges Dutch to Match Insurgent's US Sentence*, Associated Press, Apr. 15, 2009.[56] Nevertheless, the government views the conviction as a victory, with U.S. Attorney Jeffrey A. Taylor stating that "[t]his case, which represents the first use of the United States criminal courts to prosecute an individual for terrorism offenses against Americans in Iraq, demonstrates our resolve to use every tool at our disposal to defend Americans, both at home and abroad." Press Release, U.S. Dep't of Justice, Iraqi-Born Dutch Citizen Sentenced to 25 Years in Prison for Terrorism Conspiracy Against Americans in Iraq (Apr. 16, 2009).[57] While the *al-Delaema* case illustrates that cooperation and often compromise will be required in order to prosecute foreign citizens in the American court system, it also demonstrates a willingness on the part of foreign governments to entrust their citizens to the American court system for trial and, to a degree, for sentence in terrorism cases. It is not self-evident that other countries will cooperate to the same extent or extradite their citizens for proceedings in which the defendant's rights would be curtailed as has been proposed in a new national security court or in military commissions.

IX.
Safety and Security of Communities Near Prisons Holding Terrorism Defendants

In *In Pursuit of Justice*, we examined the ability of the federal criminal justice system to assure the safety and security of the judges, jurors, and witnesses, as well as the ability of the Bureau of Prisons to maintain security within the prison system. *See In Pursuit of Justice*, at 121-27. While terrorism cases have tested the system and its resources, and there has been at least one tragic incident in which a prison guard was severely injured, *see id.* at 121 (detailing the attack on Louis Pepe by Mamdouh Mahmud Salim), we concluded that in general the justice system was able to manage the security challenges of terrorism cases, and indeed has been doing so for more than twenty years. As terrorism prosecutions have continued in the past year, the security issues posed by terrorism prosecutions have continued to be managed successfully within the Article III courts and the Bureau of Prisons.

As it has in other areas of the terrorism debate, Guantánamo, with its over 200 detainees, has provoked new questions about safety and security. The current debate has focused on the capacity of the court system and U.S. prisons to protect the safety and security of the communities to which the detainees will be sent to be detained pending trial and beyond, if they are convicted. The debate has largely been driven by elected representatives from around the country who have objected to the prospect of Guantánamo detainees being incarcerated in correctional facilities in their

districts. *See, e.g.*, David D. Kirkpatrick & David M. Herszenhorn, *Guantánamo Hands G.O.P. A Wedge Issue*, N.Y. Times, May 24, 2009, at A1[58] (Kansas Senator Pat Roberts opposing any transfer of Guantánamo detainees to the maximum security facility in Ft. Leavenworth, Kansas); *Sen. Hatch Opposes Closing Guantánamo, Transferring Enemy Combatants to U.S.*, US Fed. News, Mar. 13, 2009[59] (quoting Sen. Hatch as stating "Bringing these detainees to the continental United States is tantamount to injecting a virus into a healthy body" and characterizing the availability of maximum security prison space within the federal prison system as inadequate if the U.S. is unable to place these detainees into the custody of other countries); Mike Sunnucks, *Rep. Trent Franks looks to keep Guantánamo prisoners out of Arizona*, Phoenix Bus. J., Feb. 10, 2009[60] (discussing efforts of Congressman Trent Franks of Arizona and several state senators to introduce legislation to prohibit Guantánamo detainees from being transferred to federal prisons or military bases in Arizona); Charles Hurt & Carl Campanile, *'The Terrorists Will Now Cheer'* , N.Y. Post, Jan. 23, 2009[61] (quoting New York Congressman Peter King regarding transferring prisoners out of Guantánamo: "This is madness. These are hardened terrorists who should not be detained in the US. We live in a dangerous world. Guantánamo is a necessary evil."). Indeed, President Obama's plans to shut down

Guantánamo and move its detainees have met stiff resistance from Congress generally. *See* David M. Herszenhorn, *In Shift, Leaders of Senate Reject Guantánamo Aid*, N.Y. Times, May 20, 2009[62] (discussing the Senate's 90-6 vote blocking the transfer of Guantánamo detainees to the United States and denying the administration the funding for closing the facility); *see also* Supplemental Appropriations Act, 2009 Pub. L. No. 111-32 § 14103 (2009) (restricting the use of funding for transfer of detainees from the Guantánamo Bay detention facility).

On June 9, 2009, the Department of Justice issued two important press releases relating respectively to the transfer of an important Guantánamo detainee to pretrial detention in a U.S. prison and the capacity of the prison system to handle accused terrorists. The first press release announced that Ahmed Khalfan Ghailani, a Tanzanian national who had been held in Guantánamo since September 2006, had arrived that morning at the Metropolitan Correctional Center in Manhattan to face charges for his role in the 1998 bombings of the U.S. Embassies in Tanzania and Kenya. *See* Press Release, U.S. Dep't of Justice, Ahmed Ghailani Transferred from Guantánamo Bay to New York for Prosecution on Terror Charges (June 9, 2009).[63] The second press release set forth a record of the criminal justice system's long history of dealing with terrorists. *See* Press Release, U.S. Dep't of Justice, Fact Sheet: Prosecuting and Detaining Terror Suspects in the U.S. Criminal Justice System (June 9, 2009).[64] The second press release does not mention the roiled debate over the safety and security issues of bringing Guantánamo detainees to the United States, but it seems designed to address it by marshaling facts regarding the justice system's successful efforts in prosecuting and incarcerating convicted terrorists. *See id.* It lays out the record of the U.S. Attorney's Office for the Southern District of New York in prosecuting major terrorism cases, as well as recent cases in 2008 and 2009 prosecuted by that office. *See id.* The press release then provides important

statistics which give some context to how many terrorists are already detained in the federal prison system, even before any Guantánamo detainees are counted. *See id.* According to the release, "[t]here are currently 216 inmates in Bureau of Prisons (BOP) custody who have a history of/or nexus to international terrorism." *Id.*[65] After providing detail on the number of these prisoners who were extradited, not extradited, and who are citizens, the press release provides information on the facilities in which these individuals have been housed:

> The "Supermax" facility in Florence, Colo. (ADX Florence), which is BOP's most secure facility, houses 33 of these international terrorists. There has never been an escape from ADX Florence, and BOP has housed some of these international terrorists since the early 1990s. In addition to the ADX Florence, the BOP houses such individuals in the Communications Management Units at Terre Haute, Ind., and Marion, Ill., as well as in other facilities among different institutions around the country.

Id. The press release then also lists prominent terrorists who are currently incarcerated in BOP prisons and discusses the availability of Special Administrative Measures (SAMs), which it points out "can be initiated to prevent acts of terrorism, acts of violence, or the disclosure of classified information." *Id.*[66]

The press release seems aimed at assuaging some of the fear that has been stoked about the safety of prosecuting terrorist suspects due to the unique effect Guantánamo has had on this issue. The press release does so by providing facts that demonstrate what was already well-known to many: the U.S. justice system has a long and successful history of prosecuting suspected terrorists by generally achieving just results without causing danger to the nation's or local communities' safety and security.

The upsurge of "NIMBY" (i.e., "not in my back yard") refusals by some elected representatives to receive detainees for prosecution, or potentially military detention, appears to be based mainly on fears being fanned rather than facts being aired. While it is no small matter to receive dangerous accused terrorists in any district, and must be treated with the utmost seriousness, detaining accused and convicted terrorists in U.S. prisons has been done on a continuous basis since at least the early 1990s without harm to the surrounding communities. Nor are the accused terrorists in Guantánamo a breed apart from the terrorists who have been detained and remain detained in the United States. Certainly, Guantánamo detainees such as Khalid Sheikh Mohammed and Ramzi bin al-Shibh are infamous accused terrorists, but we believe they are no more threatening by their potential presence in a U.S. prison than Ramzi Yousef; the "Blind Sheikh" Omar Abdel Rahman; the "Millenium Bomber" Ahmed Ressam; Wadih el-Hage, one of the U.S. Embassy bombers; the "Shoe Bomber" Richard Reid; Zacarias Moussaoui; and Ali Saleh Kahlah al-Marri, all of whom were held in custody in U.S. prisons in various parts of the country before their convictions and are serving their sentences. Some of these defendants have already been incarcerated for approximately fifteen years. *See In Pursuit of Justice*, at 14-17. Therefore, there seems to be little empirical basis for treating the prospect of Guantánamo detainees being transferred to facilities in the United States as creating a security problem for which there is no precedent or past experience to guide our government officials.

X.
Conclusion

In the year since *In Pursuit of Justice* was released, the dread specter of terrorism continues to blight societies and afflict people around the globe. On a daily basis, the U.S. government confronts the challenge of remorseless extremists seeking to unleash horror on our citizens and our land. Our country has deployed a broad array of its powers—military, intelligence, diplomatic, economic, cultural, and law enforcement—to combat this threat.

It may well be that the struggle against terrorism will be the defining conflict of this generation. This is not simply because of the threat it poses to our country but because of the threat it poses to our national character. That terrorism must be met with an iron resolve cannot be disputed, but terrorism's unconventional nature has caused us to question how our Nation channels that resolve. Regarding our Nation's criminal justice system, there continues to be vigorous debate about creating new systems for accused terrorists. Some have argued for a "national security court"—with untested rules and procedures—to be used to try suspected terrorists, according them a different form of due process than other defendants at the bar of American justice. Similarly, some argue that, for the sake of our safety, suspected terrorists need to be able to be detained without being charged—by any measure a profound change to the nature of our legal system. Well-intentioned people can argue these issues with passion and force, but it cannot be argued that these proposed steps would not change the character of our criminal justice system.

In the past year, our country has learned that new systems, such as the Guantánamo military commissions, are more easily conceived than carried out. And in fact, wrong choices not only fail to meet their objectives, but they can affirmatively damage our Nation's standing in the world. When we damage our moral standing in the world, we risk increasing the danger to our Nation. Yet in the past year, while new systems have failed and new "fixes" have been floated, the criminal justice system has continued to build on its long record of being an effective and fair tool for incapacitating terrorists. The evidence collected in this 2009 Report confirms what was demonstrated in *In Pursuit of Justice*; that is, that the justice system, while not perfect, continues to adapt to handle all manner of terrorism prosecutions without sacrificing our national security interests or our commitment to fairness and due process for all. As we move forward, using all our available military, intelligence, diplomatic, and economic resources, we should continue with confidence to call upon the criminal justice system as a potent tool to combat terrorism and to demonstrate the character of American justice.

Appendix A:
Terrorism Prosecution Cases

1. United States v. Abdhir, No. 5:07-cr-00501-JF (N.D. Cal. Aug. 1, 2007)

2. United States v. Abdi, No. 1:01-cr-00404-TSE (E.D. Va. Oct. 23, 2001)

3. United States v. Abdi, No. 2:04-cr-00088-ALM (S.D. Ohio June 10, 2004)

4. United States v. Abdoulah, No. 3:01-cr-03240-TJW (S.D. Cal. Nov. 2, 2001)

5. United States v. Abdulah, No. 2:01-cr-00977-PGR (D. Ariz. Oct. 25, 2001) (related cases: No. 2:02-cr-00164-PGR (D. Ariz. Feb. 20, 2002) and No. 2:02-cr-00004-UA (C.D.Cal. Jan. 3, 2002))

6. United States v. Abu Ali, No. 1:05-cr-00053-GBL (E.D. Va. Feb. 3, 2005)

7. United States v. Abuali, No. 2:01-cr-00686-WHW (D.N.J. Oct. 25, 2001)

8. United States v. Abu-Jihaad, No. 3:07-cr-00057-MRK (D. Conn. Mar. 21, 2007)

9. United States v. Afshari, No. 2:01-cr-00209-RMT (C.D. Cal. Feb. 26, 2001)

10. United States v. Ahmad, No. 3:04-cr-00301-MRK (D. Conn. Oct. 6, 2004)

11. United States v. Ahmed, No. 1:06-cr-00147-CC-GGB (N.D. Ga. Mar. 23, 2006)

12. United States v. Ahmed, No. 1:07-cr-00647-JGC (N.D. Ohio Dec. 13, 2007)*

13. United States v. Ahsan, No. 3:06-cr-00194-JCH (D. Conn. June 28, 2006)

14. United States v. Akhdar, No. 2:03-cr-80079-GCS (E.D. Mich. Feb. 3, 2003)

15. United States v. Alamoudi, No. 1:03-cr-00513-CMH (E.D. Va. Oct. 10, 2003)

16. United States v. al-Arian, No. 8:03-cr-00077-JSM-TBM (M.D. Fla. Feb. 19, 2003)

17. United States v. al-Delaema, No. 1:05-cr-00337-PLF (D.D.C. Sept. 9, 2005)*

18. United States v. al-Draibi, No. 1:01-cr-00393-TSE (E.D. Va. Oct. 10, 2001)

19. United States v. Alfauri, No. 1:02-cr-00147-TSE (E.D. Va. Apr. 10, 2002)

20. United States v. al-Hussayen, No. 3:03-cr-00048-EJL (D. Idaho Feb. 13, 2003)

21. United States v. Alishtari, No. 1:07-cr-00115-AKH (S.D.N.Y. Feb. 14, 2007)

22. United States v. al-Marri, No. 1:03-cr-10044-MMM (C.D. Ill. May 22, 2003) (related cases: No. 1:02-cr-00147-VM (S.D.N.Y. Feb. 6, 2002); No. 1:03-cr-00094-VM (S.D.N.Y. Jan. 22, 2003)); and No. 1:09-cr-10030-MMM-JAG-1 (C.D. Ill. Feb. 26, 2009)*

23. United States v. al-Moayad, No. 1:03-cr-01322-SJ (E.D.N.Y. Dec. 15, 2003)

24. United States v. al-Mughassil, No. 1:01-cr-00228-CMH (E.D. Va. June 21, 2001)

25. United States v. Alrababah, No. 1:02-cr-00096-GBL (E.D.Va. Nov. 16, 2001)

26. United States v. al-Timimi, No. 1:04-cr-00385-LMB (E.D. Va. Sept. 23, 2004)

27. United States v. Amawi, No. 3:06-cr-00719-JGC (N.D. Ohio Feb. 16, 2006)

28. United States v. Aref, No. 1:04-cr-00402-TJM (N.D.N.Y. Aug. 6, 2004)

29. United States v. Arnaout, No. 1:02-cr-00892-SBC (N.D. Ill. Oct. 9, 2002) (related case: No. 1:02-cr-00414-JBG (N.D. Ill. May 29, 2002))

30. United States v. Assi, No. 2:98-cr-80695-GER (E.D. Mich. Aug. 4, 1998)

31. United States v. Awadallah, No. 1:01-cr-01026-SAS (S.D.N.Y. Oct. 31, 2001)

32. United States v. Awan, No. 1:06-cr-00154-CPS-VVP (S.D.N.Y. Mar. 10, 2006)

33. United States v. Azmath, No. 1:02-cr-00045-SAS (S.D.N.Y. Jan. 14, 2002)

34. United States v. Babar, No. 1:04-cr-00528-VM (S.D.N.Y. June 2, 2004)

35. United States v. Badri, No. 4:01-cr-0323-FJG (W.D. Mo. Nov. 14, 2001)

36. United States v. Batiste, No. 1:06-cr-20373-JAL (S.D. Fla. June 22, 2006) (the "Liberty City Seven" case)

37. United States v. Battle, No. 3:02-cr-00399-JO (D. Or. Oct. 3, 2002)

38. United States v. Benevolence International Foundation, No. 1:02-cr-00414-JBG (N.D. Ill. May 29, 2002)

39. United States v. Benkahla, No. 1:06-cr-00009-JCC (E.D. Va. Feb. 9, 2006)

40. United States v. Biheiri, No. 1:03-cr-00365-TSE (E.D. Va. Aug. 7, 2003)

41. United States v. Budiman, No. 1:02-cr-00074-GBL (E.D. Va. Feb. 21, 2002)

42. United States v. Chandia, No. 1:05-cr-00401-CMH (E.D. Va. Sept. 14, 2005)

43. United States v. Cromitie, No. 7:09-cr-00558-CM (S.D.N.Y. June 2, 2009)*

44. United States v. Damrah, No. 1:03-cr-00484-JG (N.D. Ohio Dec. 16, 2003)

45. United States v. Defreitas, No. 1:07-cr-00543-DLI (E.D.N.Y. June 28, 2007)

46. United States v. Doha, No. 1:01-cr-00832-RWS (S.D.N.Y. Aug. 27, 2002)

47. United States v. Dumeisi, No. 1:03-cr-00664-SBC (N.D. Ill. July 16, 2003)

48. United States v. Elashi, No. 3:02-cr-00052-SAL (N.D. Tex. Feb. 20, 2002)

49. United States v. Elfgeeh, No. 1:03-cr-00133-SJ (E.D.N.Y. Feb. 3, 2003)

50. United States v. el-Gabrowny, No. 1:93-cr-00181-MBM (S.D.N.Y. Mar. 17, 1993) (the "Sheikh Abdel Rahman/Landmarks and Tunnels" case)

51. United States v. el-Hage, No. 1:98-cr-01023-KTD (S.D.N.Y. Sept. 21, 1998) (the "Embassy Bombings" case)

52. United States v. el-Jassem, No. 1:73-cr-00500-JBW (E.D.N.Y. Mar. 17, 1973) (related case: United States v. al-Jawary, No. 1:73-cr-00481-UA (S.D.N.Y. May 23, 1973))

53. United States v. Elzahabi, No. 0:04-cr-00282-JRT-FLN-1 (D. Minn. July 7, 2004)*

54. United States v. Faris, No. 1:03-cr-00189-LMB (E.D. Va. Apr. 30, 2003)

55. United States v. Gadahn, No. 8:05-cr-00254-UA (C.D. Cal. Oct. 12, 2005)

56. United States v. Galicia, No. 1:01-cr-00411-LMB (E.D. Va. Oct. 25, 2001)

57. United States v. Goba, No. 1:02-cr-00214-WMS-HKS (W.D.N.Y. Oct. 21, 2002) (the "Lackawanna Six" case)

58. United States v. Grecula, No. 4:05-cr-00257-KPE (S.D. Tex. June 16, 2005)

59. United States v. Hamed, No. 1:02-cr-00082-JCC (E.D. Va. Feb. 26, 2002)

60. United States v. Hammoud, No. 3:00-cr-00147-GCM-CH (W.D.N.C. July 31, 2000)

61. United States v. Haouari, No. 1:00-cr-00015-JFK (S.D.N.Y. Jan. 19, 2000)

62. United States v. Hashmi, No. 1:06-cr-00442-LAP (S.D.N.Y. May 24, 2006)

63. United States v. Hassan, No. 1:03-cr-00171-SJ (E.D.N.Y. Feb. 13, 2003)

64. United States v. Hassoun, No. 0:04-cr-60001-MGC (S.D. Fla. Jan. 8, 2004) (the "Jose Padilla" case)

65. United States v. Hayat, No. 2:05-cr-00240-GEB (E.D. Cal. June 16, 2005)

66. United States v. Holy Land Foundation for Relief and Development, No. 3:04-cr-00240-JAS (N.D. Tex. July 26, 2004)

67. United States v. Hussain, No. 2:01-cr-01328-JS (E.D.N.Y. Dec. 4, 2001)

68. United States v. Hussein, No. 1:01-cr-10423-REK (D. Mass. Nov. 14, 2001)

69. United States v. Islamic American Relief Agency, No. 4:07-cr-00087-NKL (W.D. Mo. Mar. 6, 2007)

70. United States v. Idris, No. 1:02-cr-00306-CMH (E.D. Va. Mar. 21, 2002)

71. United States v. Iqbal, No. 1:06-cr-01054-RMB (S.D.N.Y. Nov. 15, 2006)

72. United States v. Isse, No. 1:02-cr-00142-JCC (E.D. Va. Apr. 3, 2002)

73. United States v. Jabarah, No. 1:02-cr-01560-BSJ (S.D.N.Y. Dec. 12, 2002)

74. United States v. Jaber, No. 5:05-cr-50030-JLH (W.D. Ark. Aug. 11, 2005)

75. United States v. James, No. 8:05-cr-00214-CJC (C.D. Cal. Aug. 31, 2005)

76. United States v. Janjalani, No. 1:02-cr-00068 (D.D.C. Feb. 12, 2002)

77. United States v. Khadr, No. 1:06-cr-10028-GAO (D. Mass. Feb. 28, 2006)

78. United States v. Khan, No. 1:08-cr-00621-NRB (S.D.N.Y. July 8, 2008)*

79. United States v. Lafi Khalil, No. 1:99-cr-01134-JBW (E.D.N.Y. Dec. 14, 1999)

80. United States v. Naji Khalil, No. 1:04-cr-00573-GBD (S.D.N.Y. June 17, 2004) (related case: No. 4:05-cr-00200-GH (E.D. Ark. July 26, 2005))

81. United States v. Khoury, No. 4:01-cr-00751-DH (S.D. Tex. Oct. 3, 2001)

82. United States v. Mustafa Kilfat, No. 2:01-cr-00792-AMW (D.N.J. Dec. 11, 2001)

83. United States v. Ahmad Kilfat, No. 2:01-cr-00793-AMW (D.N.J. Dec. 11, 2001)

84. United States v. Koubriti, No. 2:01-cr-80778-GER (E.D. Mich. Sept. 27, 2001) (the "Detroit Sleeper Cell" case)

85. United States v. Kourani, No. 2:03-cr-81030-RHC-RSW (E.D. Mich. Jan. 15, 2004)

86. United States v. Lakhani, No. 2:03-cr-00880-KSH (D.N.J. Dec. 18, 2003)

87. United States v. Lindh, No. 1:02-cr-00037-TSE (E.D. Va. Feb. 5, 2002)

88. United States v. Lopez-Flores, No. 1:01-cr-00430-GBL (E.D. Va. Oct. 24, 2001)

89. United States v. Maflahi, No. 1:03-cr-00412-NG (E.D.N.Y. Apr. 9, 2003)

90. United States v. Maldonado, No. 4:07-cr-00124-GHM (S.D. Tex. Apr. 2, 2007)

91. United States v. Mandhai, No. 0:02-cr-60096-WPD (S.D. Fla. May. 16, 2002)

92. United States v. Martinez-Flores, No. 1:01-cr-00412-TSE (E.D. Va. Oct. 25, 2001)

93. United States v. Marzook, No. 1:03-cr-00978 (N.D. Ill. Oct. 9, 2003)

94. United States v. Mehanna, No. 1:09-cr-10017-GAO (D. Mass. Jan. 15, 2009)*

95. United States v. Mohammed, No. 1:06-cr-00357-CKK-1 (D.D.C. Dec. 13, 2006)*

96. United States v. Moussaoui, No. 1:01-cr-00455-LMB (E.D. Va. Dec. 11, 2001)

97. United States v. Mubayyid, No. 4:05-cr-40026-FDS (D. Mass. May 11, 2005)

98. United States v. Mustafa, No. 1:04-cr-00356-JFK (S.D.N.Y. Apr. 19, 2004)

99. United States v. Niazi, No. 8:09-cr-00028-CJC (C.D. Cal. Feb. 11, 2009)*

100. United States v. Noman, No. 2:02-cr-00431-JWB (D.N.J. May 21, 2002)

101. United States v. Noorzai, No. 1:05-cr-00019-DC-1 (S.D.N.Y. Jan 6, 2005)*

102. United States v. Obeid, No. 3:05-cr-00149-TMR (S.D. Ohio Oct. 25, 2005)

103. United States v. Paracha, No. 1:03-cr-01197-SHS (S.D.N.Y. Oct. 8, 2003)

104. United States v. Paul, No. 2:07-cr-00087-GLF (S.D. Ohio Apr. 11, 2007)

105. United States v. Pervez, No. 1:02-cr-00174-JES (S.D.N.Y. Feb. 13, 2002)

106. United States v. Qureshi, No. 6:04-cr-60057-RFD-CMH (W.D. La. Oct. 13, 2004)

107. United States v. Rahimi, No. 1:03-cr-00486-DC (S.D.N.Y. April 17, 2003)*

108. United States v. Raissi, No. 2:01-cr-00911-EHC (D. Ariz. Oct. 9, 2001) (related case: No. 2:01-cr-01075-SRB (D. Ariz. Nov. 27, 2001))

109. United States v. Ranjha, No. 1:07-cr-00239-MJG (D. Md. May 23, 2007)

110. United States v. Ranson, No. 3:05-cr-00016-TSL-JCS (S. D. Miss. Feb. 18, 2005)

111. United States v. Rashed, No. 1:87-cr-00308-RCL (D.D.C. July 14, 1987)

112. Unites States v. Ressam, No. 99-cr-00666-JCC (W.D. Wash. Dec. 22, 1999) (the "Millenium Bomber" case)

113. United States v. Reid, No. 1:02-cr-10013-WGY (D. Mass. Jan. 16, 2002) (the "Shoe Bomber" case)

114. United States v. Rezaq, No. 1:93-cr-00284-RCL (D.D.C. July 15, 1993)

115. United States v. Rizvi, No. 1:01-cr-00418-WDM (D. Colo. Nov. 28, 2001)

116. United States v. Royer, No. 1:03-cr-00296-LMB (E.D. Va. June 25, 2003) (the "Virginia Jihad Network" case)

117. United States v. Salameh, No. 1:93-cr-00180-KTD (S.D.N.Y. Mar. 17, 1993) (the "World Trade Center I" and "Bojinka Plot" case)

118. United States v. Salim, No. 1:01-cr-00002-DAB (S.D.N.Y. Jan. 3, 2001)

119. United States v. Sattar, No. 1:02-cr-00395-JGK (S.D.N.Y. Apr. 9, 2002) (the "Lynne Stewart" case)

120. United States v. Serif Mohamed, No. 8:07-cr-00342-SDM-MAP (M.D. Fla. Aug. 29, 2007)

121. United States v. Tarik Shah, No. 1:05-cr-00673-LAP (S.D.N.Y. June 27, 2005)

122. United States v. Syed Shah, No. 3:02-cr-02912-MJL (S.D. Cal. Oct. 30, 2002)

123. United States v. Shannaq, No. 1:02-cr-00319-AMD (D. Md. July 2, 2002)

124. Unites States v. Shareef, No. 1:06-cr-00919 (N.D. Ill. Dec. 8, 2006)*

125. United States v. Shnewer, No. 1:07-cr-00459-RBK (D.N.J. June 5, 2007) (the "Fort Dix Plot" case)

126. United States v. Siddiqui, No. 1:08-cr-00826-RMB-1 (S.D.N.Y. Sept. 2, 2008)*

127. United States v. Siraj, No. 1:05-cr-00104-NG (E.D.N.Y. Feb. 9, 2005)

128. United States v. Subeh, No. 6:04-cr-06077-CJS-MWP (W.D.N.Y. Apr. 22, 2004)

129. United States v. Tabatabai, No. 2:99-cr-00225-CAS (C.D. Cal. Mar. 10, 1999)

130. United States v. Taleb-Jedi, No. 1:06-cr-00652-BMC (E.D.N.Y. Sept. 29, 2006)

131. United States v. Ujaama, No. 2:02-cr-00283-BJR (W.D. Wash. Aug. 28, 2002)

132. United States v. Villalobos, No. 1:01-cr-00399-GBL (E.D. Va. Oct. 17, 2001)

133. United States v. Walker, No. 3:04-cr-02701-DB (W.D. Tex. Dec. 8, 2004)

134. United States v. Warsame, No. 0:04-cr-00029-JRT-FLN (D. Minn. Jan. 20, 2004)

135. United States v. Yunis, No. 1:87-cr-00377 (D.D.C. Sept. 15, 1987)

Endnotes

[1] *Available at* http://www.humanrightsfirst.info/pdf/080521-USLS-pursuit-justice.pdf. *In Pursuit of Justice* is also referred to herein as the "White Paper." In this 2009 Report, page number references to the White Paper are to the version available at the link above.

[2] Review and Disposition of Individuals Detained at the Guantánamo Bay Naval Base and Closure of Detention Facilities, Exec. Order No. 13,492, 74 Fed. Reg. 4,897 (Jan. 22, 2009); Review of Detention Policy Options, Exec. Order No. 13,493, 74 Fed. Reg. 4,901 (Jan. 22, 2009).

[3] *See* Barack Obama, U.S. President, Statement of President Barack Obama on Military Commissions (May 15, 2009), *available at* http://www.whitehouse.gov/the_press_office/Statement-of-President-Barack-Obama-on-Military-Commissions; Barack Obama, U.S. President, Remarks by the President on National Security (May 21, 2009), *available at* http://www.whitehouse.gov/the_press_office/Remarks-by-the-President-On-National-Security-5-21-09.

[4] Remarks by the President on National Security (May 21, 2009).

[5] *Compare* The Constitution Project, Liberty and Sec. Comm. & Coalition to Defend Checks and Balances, *A Critique of "National Security Courts"* (June 23, 2008), *available at* http://www.constitutionproject.org/pdf/Critique_of_the_National_Security_Courts.pdf (arguing in favor of capability of criminal justice system to handle terrorism cases); Hon. Leonie Brinkema, Address at the Am. U. Washington College of Law/Brookings Institution Conference: "Terrorists and Detainees: Do We Need A New National Security Court," (Feb. 1, 2008), *audio available at* http://www.wcl.american.edu/podcast/ audio/20080201_WCL_TAD.mp3 (same); *with* Kevin E. Lunday & Harvey Rishikof, *Due Process Is a Strategic Choice: Legitimacy and the Establishment of an Article III National Security Court*, 39 Cal. W. Int'l L.J. 87 (2008) (arguing in favor of national security courts); Jack Goldsmith, *Long-Term Terrorist Detention and Our National Security Court*, (Series on Counterterrorism and American Statutory Law, Working Paper No. 5, 2009), *available at* http://www.brookings.edu/~/media/files/rc/papers/2009/0209_detention_goldsmith/0209_detention_goldsmith.pdf (same); Benjamin Wittes, *Law and the Long War: The Future of Justice in the Age of Terror* (Penguin Press 2008) (same); Amos N. Guiora & John T. Parry, *Light at the End of the Pipeline?: Choosing a Forum for Suspected Terrorists*, 156 U. Pa. L. Rev. PENNumbra 356 (2008) (same). In a forthcoming symposium essay, Professor Robert Chesney concludes that many of the leading criticisms of the capability of the criminal justice system regarding terrorism are overstated, but notes "three sets of procedural safeguards that do tend to limit the reach of the criminal justice system in comparison to existing or proposed alternatives" and discusses "modest steps Congress might take to optimize the criminal justice system for the task of prevention-oriented prosecution." Robert M. Chesney, *Terrorism, Criminal Prosecution, and the Preventive Detention Debate* (working draft) at 2, forthcoming, S. Tex. L. Rev., *available at* http://papers.ssrn.com/sol3/papers.cfm?abstract_id=1306733. For a useful summary and trenchant critique of national-security-court proposals, see Stephen I. Vladek, *The Case Against National Security Courts*, 45 Willamette L. Rev. 505 (2009). Benjamin Wittes and Colleen A. Peppard of the Brookings Institution have recently issued a detailed procedural blueprint for new statutory detention authority that would supplement existing legal grounds for detaining alleged terrorists. *See* Benjamin Wittes & Colleen A. Peppard, *Designing Detention: A Model Law for Terrorist Incapacitation* (Governance Studies at Brookings 2009), *available at* http://www.brookings.edu/~/media/Files/rc/papers/2009/0626_detention_wittes/0626_detention_wittes.pdf. We summarize the Wittes/Peppard proposal below in note 33.

[6] Even with the Obama Administration's effort to develop a military commission system that will withstand constitutional challenge, there appear to be divisions over the extent to which detainees must be afforded constitutional rights. For example, it has been reported that based on legal guidance issued by the Department of Justice's Office of Legal Counsel, detainees have a constitutional right to protection against the use of statements taken through coercive interrogations. *See* Jess Bravin, *New Rift Opens Over Rights of Detainees*, Wall St. J., June 29, 2009, at A1, *available at* http://online.wsj.com/article_email/SB124623153856866179-IMyQjAxMDI5NDI2ODIyMzgxWj.html; David Johnston, *New Guidance Issued on Military Trials of Detainees*, N.Y. Times, June 29, 2009, at A14, *online version available at* http://www.nytimes.com/2009/06/29/us/29gitmo.html. That view, however, is reportedly not shared by the Department of Defense. *See* Bravin, *New Rift Opens Over Rights of Detainees*.

[7] As reported in the White Paper, there were 107 terrorism cases filed and 257 defendants charged between September 11, 2001, and December 31, 2007. *See In Pursuit of Justice*, at 23.

[8] Consistent with this approach, we have treated the cases filed against Ali Saleh Kahlah al-Marri as a single case for statistical purposes. The government initially filed charges against al-Marri in 2003 in the Central District of Illinois, but moved to dismiss the charges in order to transfer al-Marri to military custody. *Al-Marri v. Pucciarelli*, 534 F3d 213, 219 (4th Cir. 2008); *see also In Pursuit of Justice*, at 73. In February 2009, al-Marri was transferred from military custody back into the criminal justice system, and the government filed new charges against him. *See* Indictment, *United States v. al-Marri*, No. 09-cr-10030 (C.D. Ill. Feb. 26, 2009) (Dkt. No. 3). We have treated these two prosecutions as a single case in our quantitative analysis. For further explanation of the procedural history regarding al-Marri, *see infra* at 14, 20-21.

Similarly, we have treated the prosecutions of Khalil Ahmed and Zubair Ahmed as a single case in our data set. In 2007, the government charged the Chicago cousins and three co-defendants with conspiring to murder or maim American military forces abroad. *See* Superseding Indictment, *United States v. Amawi*, No. 06-cr-00719 (N.D. Ohio Feb. 7, 2007) (Dkt. No. 186). On December 13 2007, a grand jury separately indicted the Ahmed defendants for conspiracy and material support offenses that included or arose from conduct charged in the *Amawi* indictment, but also included broader conduct. *See* Indictment, *United States v. Ahmed*, No. 07-cr-00647 (N.D. Ohio Dec. 13, 2007) (Dkt. No. 1). The government moved to dismiss the Ahmed defendants from the *Amawi* case in order to proceed against them in the separate indictment, which the court granted. *See* Order, *Amawi* (N.D. Ohio Dec. 27, 2007) (Dkt. No. 525). We view these prosecutions as a single case for purposes of our quantitative analysis.

[9] Because we have re-evaluated the data going back to September 11, 2001, there are slight changes in historical data for some years as compared to the data that was presented in the White Paper.

[10] In the White Paper, we reported that 203 defendants were arrested and subjected to a bail determination in cases filed between September 11, 2001, and December 31, 2007, and that 139 of these defendants were detained while 70 defendants were released on conditions. *See In Pursuit of Justice*, at 24.

[11] We have not counted the charges as "resolved" where they were dismissed prior to arraignment because we do not believe useful inferences about the efficacy of the justice system can be drawn from the dismissal in this circumstance. There are two such cases in the overall data set. First, the government dismissed the charges against Habis al-Saoub in *United States v. Battle* after al-Saoub was killed in Afghanistan but before he was arraigned in court. *See* Order, No. 02-cr-00399 (D. Or. July 1, 2004) (Dkt. No. 430); Fed. Bureau of Investigation, The Portland Division: A Brief History, http://portland.fbi.gov/history.htm (last visited July 23, 2009). This outcome, commonly known as a "death nolle," does not in our view provide any useful way to assess the success of the prosecution. Second, the government dismissed the charges against an organization called Hamza, Inc. in *United States v. Ranjha* after the individual defendants pled guilty but before Hamza, Inc. was arraigned. *See* Docket, 07-cr-00239 (D. Md.). Again, the dismissal prior to arraignment does not in our view provide meaningful information about the success or failure of the prosecution, especially because Hamza, Inc. was a corporation rather than an individual.

[12] In the White Paper, we reported that 97 defendants still had charges pending while all charges were resolved for 160 defendants. *See In Pursuit of Justice*, at 26.

[13] The 19 defendants for whom all charges were resolved by acquittal or dismissal are the following: Abdullahi Jama Amir, *United States v. Abdoulah*, No. 01-cr-03240 (S.D. Cal.); Sameeh Taha Hammoudeh, *United States v. al-Arian*, No. 03-cr-00077 (M.D. Fla.); Ghassan Zayed Ballut, *United States v. al-Arian*, No. 03-cr-00077 (M.D. Fla.); Sami Omar al-Hussayen, *United States v. al-Hussayen*, No. 03-cr-00048 (D. Idaho); Benevolence International Foundation Inc., *United States v. Arnaout*, No. 02-cr-00892 (N.D. Ill.) and *United States v. Benevolence International Foundation Inc.*, No. 02-cr-00414 (N.D. Ill.); Osama Awadallah, *United States v. Awadallah*, No. 01-cr-01026 (S.D.N.Y.); Naudimar Herrera, *United States v. Batiste*, No. 06-cr-20373 (S.D. Fla.); Lyglenson Lemorin, *United States v. Batiste*, No. 06-cr-20373 (S.D. Fla.); Enaam Arnout, *United States v. Benevolence International Foundation Inc.*, No. 02-cr-00414 (N.D. Ill.); Isahn Elashi, *United States v. Elashi*, No. 02-cr-00052 (N.D. Tex.); Farouk Ali-Hammoud, *United States v. Koubriti*, No. 01-cr-80778 (E.D. Mich.); Abdel Ilah Elmardoudi, *United States v. Koubriti*, No. 01-cr-80778 (E.D. Mich.); Youssef Megahed, *United States v. Mohamed*, No. 07-cr-00342 (M.D. Fla.); Samir al-Monla, *United States v. Mubayyid*, No. 05-cr-40026 (D. Mass); Abdur Rashid, *United States v. Rahimi*, No. 03-cr-00486 (S.D.N.Y.); Shah Wali, *United States v. Rahimi*, No. 03-cr-00486 (S.D.N.Y.); Sabri Benkhala, *United States v. Royer*, No. 03-cr-00296 (E.D. Va.); and Caliph Abdur-Raheem, *United States v. Royer*, No. 03-cr-00296 (E.D. Va.). In *Mubbayid*, al-Monla was convicted at trial of tax and false statement offenses. After trial, the district court found that the government had presented "substantial evidence at the trial that all three defendants supported and promoted jihad and the mujahideen, that is, religious-based violence and people who engage in it, through newsletters, financial donations, lectures and otherwise," but the court granted al-Monla's motion for judgment of acquittal on grounds that the prosecution was barred by the statute of limitations. *See* Tr. of Hr'g at 5, *Mubayyid* (D. Mass. June 3, 2008) (Dkt. No. 536). The government has appealed the trial court's decision.

In preparing this 2009 Report, we determined that the White Paper erroneously included one defendant, Habis al-Saoub, in the list of defendants for whom all charges were resolved by acquittal or dismissal. *See In Pursuit of Justice*, at 150 n.127. As noted above, al-Saoub was never arraigned and the charges against him were dismissed following his death in Afghanistan. *See supra* note 11.

[14] In some instances, including *Benkhala* and *Arnaout*, the subsequent charges are based on terrorism and are thus included in our data set. *See United States v. Benkhala*, No. 06-cr-00009 (E.D. Va.); *United States v. Arnaout*, No. 02-cr-00892 (N.D. Ill.). In other cases, however, the subsequent prosecutions do not meet our criteria for a demonstrated link to allegations of Islamist terrorism and thus are excluded from the data set, even though they resulted in the defendant's conviction and imprisonment or removal. *See United States v. Hammoudeh*, No. 04-cr-00330 (M.D. Fla.); *United States v. Elmardoudi*, No. 06-cr-00262 (D. Minn.). In another case, the government obtained a conviction at trial but the conviction was overturned on appeal because the Fifth Circuit determined that the government was barred from prosecuting the defendant as a result of an earlier conviction and guilty plea. *See United States v. Elashyi*, 554 F.3d 480 (5th Cir. 2008).

[15] For example, the government reportedly commenced removal proceedings against Youssef Megahed and Lyglenson Lemorin soon after their acquittals on terrorism charges. *See* Damien Cave, *Cleared of Terrorism Charges, but Then a Target for Deportation*, N.Y. Times, June 4, 2009, at A01, *online version available at* http://www.nytimes.com/2009/06/04/us/04terror.html; Peter Whoriskey, *Man Acquitted in Terror Case Faces Deportation*, Wash. Post, Mar. 2, 2008, at A03, *available at* http://www.washingtonpost.com/wp-dyn/content/article/2008/03/01/AR2008030101566.html.

[16] Sentencing data for the White Paper can be found in *In Pursuit of Justice* at page 26.

[17] In the White Paper, we reported that 23 defendants had been convicted of violating 18 U.S.C. § 1001. Since the White Paper's publication, two defendants have had their convictions for this offense vacated or dismissed by the court. *See United States v. Elashyi*, 554 F.3d 480 (5th Cir. 2008) (vacating defendant's conviction where prosecution ran afoul of prior plea agreement with defendant); *See* Tr. of Hr'g, *Mubayyid* (D. Mass. June 3, 2008) (Dkt. No. 536) (granting al-Monla's motion for judgment of acquittal).

[18] The government's continued reliance on § 2339B is hardly surprising, as "[t]he DOJ counterterrorism enforcement manual describes 2339B as 'the closest thing American prosecutors have to the crime of being a terrorist.'" Andrew Peterson, *Addressing Tomorrow's Terrorists*, 2 J. Nat'l Security L. & Pol'y 297, 301 (2008) (quoting Jeffrey A. Breinholt, *Counterterrorism Enforcement: A Lawyer's Guide* 264 (U.S. Dep't of Justice Office of Legal Educ. 2004)).

[19] The fifteen-year maximum likely represents a negotiated capped exposure that reflects the unusual history and circumstances of al-Marri's case. Indeed, if the court credits al-Marri's time in military detention against his sentence, his sentence may be less than fifteen years. *Cf.* Kirk Semple, *Padilla Gets 17-Year Term for Role in Conspiracy*, N.Y. Times, Jan. 23, 2008, at A14, *online version available at* http://www.nytimes.com/2008/01/22/us/22cnd-padilla.html (noting that sentencing judge "gave Mr. Padilla credit for time served during his 3 1/2-year detention in a South Carolina military brig"). The financial fraud, false identity, and false statements crimes with which al-Marri was originally charged, and which also exposed him to substantial penalties, *see* Indictment, *United States v. al-Marri*, No. 03-cr-00094 (S.D.N.Y. Jan. 22, 2003) (Dkt. No. 4), were dismissed with prejudice at the government's request, *see* Order, *United States v. al-Marri*, No. 03-cr-10044 (C.D. Ill. June 23, 2003) (Dkt. No. 16), when al-Marri was transferred into military custody approximately one month before his original criminal trial was scheduled to begin in 2003. *See* Scheduling Order, *al-Marri* (C.D. Ill. May 29, 2003) (Dkt. No. 7) (setting trial for July 21, 2003). Thus, those charges were no longer viable when al-Marri was returned to the criminal justice system in 2009. It is, therefore, possible that al-Marri's ultimate sentence will be less than it might have been had he been expeditiously prosecuted on the original charges that were filed against him 2002. Had the government done so, it still could have later begun a separate prosecution on material support charges, and al-Marri might well have faced an aggregate sentence longer than the one he is currently facing.

[20] *Available at* http://www.usdoj.gov/opa/pr/2009/January/09-nsd-041.html.

[21] The words "physical asset" no longer appear in the statutory definition of material support. 18 U.S.C. § 2339A(b)(1); *see also* Intelligence Reform and Terrorism Prevention Act of 2004, Pub. L. 108-458, § 6603(b), 118 Stat. 3638 (2004) (establishing most recent formulation of definition).

[22] Based on our research, both the case law and legislative history discussing the material support statutes are silent as to the applicability of these terms to the circumstances of Abu Jihaad's case. It is true that the Ninth Circuit has found the terms "service" and "specialized knowledge" (when used, as here, in a non-scientific or technical way) to be unconstitutionally vague as part of the definition of material support in § 2339B. *Humanitarian Law Project v. Mukasey*, 509 F.3d 1122, 1135-36 (9th Cir. 2007), *amended and superseded*, 552 F.3d 916 (9th Cir. 2009). Other courts, however, have held that the Ninth Circuit's vagueness ruling would not render those terms unconstitutional when applied in a § 2339A prosecution—like Abu Jihaad's—because of § 2339A's more robust mens rea requirement. *See, e.g., Amawi*, 545 F. Supp. 2d at 684 (citing *United States v. Abdi*, 498 F. Supp. 2d 1048, 1058 (S.D. Ohio 2007)).

[23] Some may view the *Abu Jihaad* decision as an example of the problems that arise in the Article III system, whether due to a gap in the statutory arsenal deployed or due to the decisions of the independent juries or judges who are the lifeblood of the system. However, as already discussed, Abu Jihaad was convicted on another count that clearly covered his conduct, and Congress may address any gap in the statute. New systems, without the maturity and breadth of statutes of the Article III system, although intended to ease the government's burden, are not necessarily an improvement and have proven unpredictable in ways that have discouraged their proponents. For example, in one of only three military commission convictions that came out of Guantánamo, that of Salim Ahmed Hamdan, Bin Laden's former driver, the results were not only lackluster but controversial in ways that would not have occurred in an Article III prosecution. Specifically, on August 6, 2008, Hamdan was acquitted on both conspiracy specifications, and was acquitted on three of eight material support specifications. *See* Press Release, U.S. Dep't of Defense, Detainee Convicted of Terrorism Charge at Military Commission Trial (Aug. 6, 2008), *available at* http://www.defenselink.mil/releases/release.aspx?releaseid=12118; *see also* William Glaberson, *Panel Convicts bin Laden Driver in Split Verdict*, N.Y. Times, Aug. 6, 2008, at A1, *available at*
http://www.nytimes.com/2008/08/07/washington/07gitmo.html. Moreover, before trial the presiding military judge had rejected a motion to dismiss the material support charges on grounds that they violated the Ex Post Facto Clause, *see* Ruling on Motion to Dismiss (Ex Post Facto), *United States v. Hamdan* (Mil. Comm'n July 14, 2008), but the validity of the material support charges was likely to be a signficant issue on appeal, *see* Glaberson, *Panel Convicts bin Laden Driver in Split Verdict*. That critical issue was never reached because of another controversial event the day after Hamdan's conviction: Hamdan received a sentence from a jury of military officers of only five and a half years, far less than he almost certainly would have received had he been convicted in an Article III court. *See* Press Release, U.S. Dep't of Defense, Hamdan Sentenced to 66 Months (Aug. 7, 2008), *available at* http://www.defenselink.mil/releases/release.aspx?releaseid=12128. Because the military judge then awarded him credit for his time in custody, Hamdan faced only six months in custody before he would be removed from the United States. This sentence was viewed as an absurdly lenient one by many who had been defenders of the military commission system. *See, e.g.,* Andrew McCarthy, *Hamdan's Disgraceful Sentence*, Nat'l Rev. Online, Aug. 7, 2008, http://corner.nationalreview.com/post/?q=MzEzYTMyZWRmNTVmNmUzM2YyZTk1NDcwNzk3ODhmODI= (calling the sentence "the worst sentence I have ever heard of" and pointing out that in comparison "[civilian court] judges . . . have shown they take terrorism seriously—they have routinely sentenced lesser players than a personal aide to bin Laden . . . to 30 and more years.") Before he completed his sentence, in November 2008, Hamdan was transported to Yemen. *See* Press Release, U.S. Dep't of Defense, Detainee Transfer Annouced (Nov. 25, 2008), *available at* http://www.defenselink.mil/releases/release.aspx?releaseid=12372; Josh White & William Branigin, *Hamdan to be Sent to Yemen*, Wash. Post, Nov. 25, 2008, at A1, *available at* http://www.washingtonpost.com/wp-dyn/content/article/2008/11/24/AR2008112403159.html.

[24] *Available at* http://www.nytimes.com/1996/11/03/world/stoning-of-afghan-adulterers-some-go-to-take-part-others-just-to-watch.html.

[25] *Available at* http://www.washingtonpost.com/wp-dyn/content/article2007/09/29/AR2007092900508.html.

[26] http://edition.cnn.com/2008/WORLD/asiapcf/08/20/pakistan.blast/index.html.

[27] *Available at* http://www.unodc.org/pdf/research/Afghanistan_Opium_Survey_2007.pdf.

[28] *Available at* http://www.washingtonpost.com/wp-dyn/content/article/2006/12/01/AR2006120101654.html.

[29] *Available at* http://www.washingtonpost.com/wp-dyn/content/article/2008/12/22/AR2008122202359.html.

[30] The United Nations report provides some history regarding the Taliban's history with heroin production:

> [T]he Taliban are again using opium to suit their interests. Between 1996 and 2000, in Taliban-controlled areas 15,000 tons of opium were produced and exported—the regime's sole source of foreign exchange at the time. In July 2000, the Taliban leader, Mullah Omar, argued that opium was against Islam and banned its cultivation (but not its export). In recent months, the Taliban have reversed their position once again and started to extract from the drug economy resources for arms, logistics and militia pay.

United Nations Office on Drugs and Crime, *Afghanistan Opium Survey 2007*, at iv.

[31] Other recent cases in which the narco-terrorism statute was not invoked, presumably because the conduct occurred prior to the enactment of the statute, have also involved the prosecution of Afghan heroin traffickers who were linked to the Taliban. *See* Indictment, *United States v. Rahimi*, No. 03-cr-00486 (S.D.N.Y. Apr. 17, 2003) (Dkt. No. 35); Indictment, *United States v. Noorzai*, No. 05-cr-00019 (S.D.N.Y. Jan. 6, 2005) (Dkt. No. 1). Baz Mohammad was the first defendant ever extradited to the United States from Afghanistan and was convicted upon his plea of guilty and sentenced to 188 months imprisonment. Judgment as to Baz Mohammad, *Rahimi* (S.D.N.Y. Oct. 11, 2007) (Dkt. No. 253); *see also* Press Release, U.S. Att'y S.D.N.Y., Heroin Kingpin—First Defendant Ever Extradited From Afghanistan—Sentenced in Manhattan Federal Court to Over 15 Years in Prison (Oct. 5, 2007), *available at* http://www.usdoj.gov/usao/nys/pressreleases/October07/bazmohammadsentencingpr.pdf. Mohammad's organization was closely aligned with the Taliban and supported them financially through his organization's heroin trafficking which was extensive in the United States. Superseding Indictment as to Baz Mohammad at 1-3, *Rahimi* (S.D.N.Y. Oct. 20, 2005) (Dkt. No. 161). In return, the Taliban provided Mohammad's

organization with protection for its opium crops, heroin laboratories, drug-transportation routes, and members and associates. *Id.* at 3. Indeed, Mohammad reportedly told co-conspirators that selling heroin in the United States was a "jihad" because it killed Americans and took their money. *Id.* at 9.

In *Noorzai*, the defendant was convicted at trial on narcotics trafficking charges, *see* Jury Verdict, *Noorzai* (S.D.N.Y. Sept. 23, 2008), and on April 30, 2009, he was sentenced to life imprisonment, *see* Judgment, *Noorzai* (S.D.N.Y. Apr. 30, 2009) (Dkt. No. 176). Interestingly, Baz Mohammad testified against Noorzai, and in addition to detailing Noorzai's heroin operations, Mohammad testified that he had been told that Noorzai was a member of the Taliban's ruling *shura* council. Gov't Sentencing Letter at 2-3, *Noorzai* (S.D.N.Y. Feb. 20, 2009) (Dkt. No. 166). Further, according to the government, Noorzai had admitted that he had provided weapons and "400 fighters" to the Taliban. *Id.* at 8. Unlike Mohammad, Noorzai was not extradited but rather was lured to the United States to demonstrate that he had valuable information which could assist the United States in Afghanistan and elsewhere in combating terrorism. *See* Bill Powell, *The Strange Case of Haji Bashar Noorzai*, Time, Feb. 19, 2007, at 28, *online version available at* http://www.time.com/time/magazine/article/0,9171,1587252,00.html. After reportedly being debriefed for days, he was told he could not return to Afghanistan and was placed under arrest. *See id.*

[32] According to recent reports, the United States is shifting its drug policy in Afghanistan away from the eradication of opium poppy fields, which had largely proved unsuccessful, and toward interdiction of drug supplies into and out of Afghanistan, as well as the prosecution of the traffickers and even corrupt government officials. *See* Rachel Donadio, *U.S. Plans New Course for Antidrug Efforts in Afghanistan*, N.Y. Times, June 27, 2009, at A12, *available at* http://www.nytimes.com/2009/06/28/world/asia/28holbrooke.html. This new policy may lead to an increase in the number of prosecutions under 21 U.S.C. § 960a.

[33] For example, Professor Jack Goldsmith argues that the debate over *whether* to preventively detain suspected terrorists is "largely a canard" and that the debate should focus on the legal framework describing *how* preventive detention should occur. *See* Jack Goldsmith, *Long-Term Terrorist Detention and Our National Security Court* 2 (Series on Counterterrorism and American Statutory Law, Working Paper No. 5, 2009), *available at* http://www.brookings.edu/~/media/files/rc/papers/2009/0209_detention_goldsmith/0209_detention_goldsmith.pdf. Concluding that the federal courts for the District of Columbia are already de facto national security courts—by virtue of the extensive Guantánamo Bay litigation taking place there—Goldsmith argues that Congress should enact procedures to govern the detention of terrorism suspects. *See id.*; *see also* Amos N. Guiora, *Military Commissions and National Security Courts After Guantánamo*, 103 Nw. U. L. Rev. Colloquy 199 (2008); Kevin E. Lunday & Harvey Rishikof, *Due Process Is a Strategic Choice: Legitimacy and the Establishment of an Article III National Security Court*, 39 Cal. W. Int'l L.J. 87 (2008).

In a detailed proposal issued in June 2009, Benjamin Wittes and Colleen Peppard of the Brookings Institution laid out proposed legislation that would establish a scheme for long-term, court-supervised detention of alleged terrorists outside the criminal justice system, the law of war, or any other established legal framework. *See* Benjamin Wittes & Colleen A. Peppard, *Designing Detention: A Model Law for Terrorist Incapacitation* (Governance Studies at Brookings 2009), *available at* http://www.brookings.edu/~/media/Files/rc/papers/2009/0626_detention_wittes/0626_detention_wittes.pdf. Wittes and Peppard propose that, as a complement to its law-of-war and criminal detention powers, the government be allowed to preventively detain any person who is neither a U.S. citizen nor a legal U.S. immigrant, if the President reasonably believes that the person is (1) "an agent of a foreign power" as that term is defined in FISA, (2) "against which Congress has authorized the use of force," and (3) "the actions of the [person] in his capacity as an agent of the foreign power pose a danger both to any person and to the interests of the United States." *Id.* at 6-13, 16; *see also id.* at 29-31 (Sections 3(a) and 4(b) of proposed legislation, setting forth criteria for detention). If the government wished to detain the person for more than fourteen days, it would have to seek approval from the U.S. District Court for the District of Columbia in an adversarial proceeding; the court could authorize further detention for no more than six months, after which the government could petition the court for an extension of the detention period for up to six additional months, and so on. *Id.* at 15-16, 20, 30-37. The detention authority would "sunset" after three years in order to force Congress to reexamine the efficacy of the authority in deciding whether to reauthorize it. *Id.* at 21, 38.

[34] *See, e.g.*, Stephen I. Vladeck, *The Case Against National Security Courts*, 45 Willamette L. Rev. 505 (2009); *see also* The Constitution Project, Liberty and Sec. Comm. & Coalition to Defend Checks and Balances, *A Critique of "National Security Courts"* (June 23, 2008); Deborah Pearlstein, *We're All Experts Now: A Security Case Against Security Detention*, 40 Case W. Res. J. Int'l L. 577 (2009).

[35] *See In Pursuit of Justice*, at 7-8, 65-75; *see also* The Constitution Project, *A Critique of "National Security Courts"*.

[36] Under the Bush Administration, the government also asserted that the detentions of Guantánamo detainees were justified by the President's Article II powers as Commander-in-Chief, but the government appeared to abandon its Article II argument in litigation after President Obama took office. *See* *Hamlily v. Obama*, 616 F. Supp. 2d 63, 66 n.1 (D.D.C. 2009).

[37] *Available at* http://www.washingtonpost.com/wp-dyn/content/article/2009/02/27/AR2009022701692.html.

[38] This tangled series of events bears an uncanny resemblance to the gyrations of the *Padilla* litigation, which are discussed at length in *In Pursuit of Justice*. *See In Pursuit of Justice*, at 72-73. In *Padilla*, the government initially held the defendant as a material witness under the criminal justice system; it then designated him as an "enemy combatant" and moved him into military detention; and then, with Supreme Court review looming, the government indicted the defendant and transferred him back to the criminal justice system, where he was convicted of serious crimes. *See id.* As with *Padilla*, the government's decision to return al-Marri to the criminal justice system put an abrupt end to the Supreme Court litigation and left us without any further guidance from the Court on whether law-of-war detention extends broadly to persons captured in the United States.

[39] It remains unclear whether *Boumediene* authorizes prisoners held outside the United States at locations other than Guantánamo to commence habeas corpus litigation in the United States. In one case brought by detainees at Bagram Airfield in Afghanistan, Judge John Bates of the U.S. District Court for the District of Columbia held that certain of the prisoners being held at Bagram could indeed challenge their detention via habeas corpus litigation in the United States. *See al-Maqaleh v. Gates*, 604 F. Supp. 2d 205, 208-09 (D.D.C. 2009). The court applied the "practical, functional analysis . . . mandated in *Boumediene*," *id.* at 232, to each habeas petitioner, inquiring into: "(1) the citizenship and status of the detainee and the adequacy of the process through which that status determination was made; (2) the nature of the sites where apprehension and then detention took place; and (3) the practical obstacles inherent in resolving the prisoner's entitlement to the writ,'" *id.* at 214-15 (quoting *Boumediene*, 128 S. Ct. at 2259). Judge Bates concluded that detainees *moved into* Afghanistan are materially no different than those moved into Guantánamo Bay, and are equally entitled to habeas review—unless the detainees in question are Afghan citizens. *Id.* at 231. For Afghans being held in their own country, the possibility of friction between the U.S. judiciary and the Afghan government proved too much of a "practical obstacle" to allow judicial review of detention. *Id.* at 229-30. Judge Bates has since stayed his ruling and granted the government leave for an interlocutory appeal to the D.C. Circuit. *Al-Maqaleh v. Gates*, --- F. Supp. 2d ---, No. 06-cv-01669, 2009 WL 1528847, at *5 (D.D.C. June 1, 2009). Given the controversial nature of the issue and the uncertainty over the proper application of the *Boumediene* standard, it is clear that the scope of *Boumediene* will continue to be debated in appellate courts and perhaps, eventually, the Supreme Court as well.

[40] In a later portion of the opinion, Judge Bates also held that the AUMF authorizes detention of those who "committed a belligerent act," noting that this language covers "any person who has directly participated in hostilities." *Hamlily*, 616 F. Supp. 2d at 70 (internal quotations omitted). Judge Bates held, however, that the government does not have authority to detain those who "directly supported hostilities." *Id.* at 77.

[41] Judge Bates concluded that the concept of "support" "evidences an importation of principles from the criminal law context" but "is simply not authorized by the AUMF itself or by the law of war." *Hamlily*, 616 F. Supp. 2d at 76.

[42] *Available at* http://www.whitehouse.gov/the_press_office/Remarks-by-the-President-On-National-Security-5-21-09.

[43] At trial, the district court employed the silent witness rule, an evidence presentation technique that limits disclosure of evidence to the judge, jury, counsel, and witnesses—and not the public. *See In Pursuit of Justice*, at 86. The Fourth Circuit expressed no opinion about whether the use of the silent witness rule would have been proper if the defendant had been provided unredacted copies of the documents. *Abu Ali*, 528 F.3d at 255 n.22.

[44] *Available at* http://article.nationalreview.com/?q=ZDQyYjEzMTg3ZDBjZTA4MzExNjU1MTE2MzkwYTRiMTc=.

[45] On May 15, 2009, President Obama announced the reform and continuation of the military commission process at Guantánamo Bay, Cuba. Press Release, Office of the White House Press Secretary (May 15, 2009). In deciding to reform rather than abandon the military commissions, President Obama was reportedly influenced by top national security aides who argued that major legal hurdles existed to prosecuting certain detainees in civilian courts, including un-*Mirandized* statements taken by the FBI in 2006 or 2007. *See* Michael D. Shear & Peter Finn, *Obama to Revamp Military Tribunals*, Wash. Post, May 16, 2009, at A1, *available at* http://www.washingtonpost.com/wp-dyn/content/article/2009/05/15/AR2009051501771.html; Carol J. Williams & Julian E. Barnes, *Critics Pounce on Obama's Tribunal Plan*, Chi. Trib., May 17, 2009, at C23, *online version available at* http://www.chicagotribune.com/news/nationworld/chi-military-tribunals_bdmay17,0,1837831.story; Evan Perez, *Miranda Issues Cloud Gitmo Cases*, Wall St. J., June 12, 2009, at A4, *available at* http://online.wsj.com/article/SB124476465967008335.html.

[46] *See also* Tr. of Combatant Status Review Tribunal Hr'g for ISN 10014 at 4-5, 7-9 (Mar. 12, 2007) (Walid Bin Attash, through personal representative, generally agreeing with the government's allegations concerning his participation in the attacks on the USS *Cole* and admitting that he "put together the plan for the operation a year and a half prior to the operation").

[47] The Supreme Court has held that failure to provide a *Miranda* warning in advance of an incriminating statement did not necessarily invalidate a later statement given after a *Miranda* warning was properly administered. *Elstad*, 470 U.S. at 314. The Court's ruling in that case, however, was predicated at least in part on the prior statement not being coerced. *Id.* at 315. As the Court explained, "absent deliberately coercive or improper tactics in obtaining the initial statement, the mere fact that a suspect has made an unwarned admission does not warrant a presumption of compulsion. A subsequent administration of *Miranda* warnings to a suspect who has given a voluntary but unwarned statement ordinarily should suffice to remove the

conditions that precluded admission of the earlier statement. In such circumstances, the finder of fact may reasonably conclude that the suspect made a rational and intelligent choice whether to waive or invoke his rights." *Id.* at 314. The Supreme Court later elaborated on when a prior statement taken in violation of *Miranda* was separate enough from a subsequent statement given after a *Miranda* warning to render the latter admissible. *Seibert*, 542 U.S. at 615. The Court explained that several factors may determine whether *Miranda* warnings delivered in between statements "could be effective enough to accomplish their object," including "the completeness and detail of the questions and answers in the first round of interrogation, the overlapping content of the two statements, the timing and setting of the first and the second, the continuity of police personnel, and the degree to which the interrogator's questions treated the second round as continuous with the first." *Id.*

[48] The administration of *Miranda* warnings to accused terrorists captured outside the United States has also sparked political controversy. On June 18, 2009, the House Permanent Select Committee on Intelligence approved an amendment to prohibit the use of funds to provide *Miranda* warnings to terrorists captured abroad. *See* H.R. Rep. No. 111-186, at 37 (2009) (recommending passage of Intelligence Authorization Act for Fiscal Year 2010, Section 504 of which would prohibit any "funds authorized to be appropriated by this Act" from being used to provide *Miranda* warnings to any non-U.S. person located outside the United States who is "(1) suspected of terrorism, associated with terrorists, or believed to have knowledge of terrorists; or (2) a detainee in the custody of the Armed Forces of the United States"); *see also* Press Release, U.S. House of Representatives Permanent Select Committee on Intelligence Minority, Hoekstra, Republicans Fault Flawed Intelligence Bill (June 19, 2009), *available at* http://intelligence.house.gov/Media/PDFS/HoekstraRelease061909.pdf. Although this amendment seems to have been motivated by an understandable desire to ensure that intelligence interrogations are effective, its scope seems overly broad and it could, if enacted, frustrate the government's ability to use probative evidence to bring dangerous terrorists to justice.

[49] Studies report that between sixty-eight percent and eighty-three percent of suspects waived their rights under *Miranda* and willingly gave statements to authorities without the assistance of counsel. *See, e.g.*, Paul G. Cassell & Bret S. Hayman, *Police Interrogation in the 1990s: An Empirical Study of the Effects of Miranda*, 43 UCLA L. Rev. 839, 859 (1996) (reporting waiver rate of 83.7%); Richard A. Leo, *Inside the Interrogation Room*, 86 J. Crim. L. & Criminology 266, 276 (1996) (reporting waiver rate of 78.29%); George C. Thomas III, *Stories About Miranda*, 102 Mich. L. Rev. 1959, 1972 (2004) (reporting waiver rate of 68%).

[50] In a footnote, Judge Diana Gribbon Motz dissented from this portion of the panel's holding. She concluded that the level of coordination between U.S. agents and their Saudi counterparts rose to the level of "'active' or 'substantial' participation" triggering application of the "joint venture" doctrine and thus the requirement that *Miranda* warnings be administered. *Abu Ali*, 528 F.3d at 230 n.6. However, Judge Motz agreed with the other two members of the panel that even if the trial court had erroneously admitted the defendant's post-arrest statements in violation of *Miranda*, the error was harmless. *Id.* at 231.

[51] With respect to the AUSA's oral warnings, the Second Circuit agreed with the district court that the warnings were sufficient under *Miranda* and rejected defendants' argument that the AUSA's testimony regarding the warnings rendered was not credible. *In re Terrorist Bombings*, 552 F.3d at 209-10. Further, the court rejected defendants' argument that the oral warnings were inadequate because "the AUSA did not apprise them of whether they could obtain legal representation under Kenyan law." *Id.* at 211. Consistent with the court's analysis of the AOR, the court explained that "the AUSA's oral warning need not have explained (1) whether and how local defense counsel could be obtained and (2) whether and how local defense counsel, once obtained, could then participate in a custodial interrogation conducted under Kenyan auspices." *Id.*

[52] In considering the prosecution's motion to conduct a pre-trial deposition under Federal Rule of Criminal Procedure 15 of a prospective government witness who resides in another country, the court in *Ahmed* expressly endorsed the procedures adopted by the *Abu Ali* court. *United States v. Ahmed*, 587 F. Supp. 2d 853, 855 (N.D. Ohio 2008) ("[I]f the government meets its burden of showing relevance and materiality [of testimony of foreign witness], it and the defendants' attorneys, with whatever assistance of the court is needed, shall implement the procedures the Fourth Circuit approved in *U.S. v. Abu Ali*, 528 F.3d 210 (4th Cir. 2008).").

[53] The Second Circuit also faulted the trial court for allowing wide-ranging testimony from Gideon Black, a survivor of a Hamas bombing in Tel Aviv that was the subject of discussion at a wedding attended by al-Anssi and al-Moayad in Yemen. *See al-Moayad*, 545 F.3d 159-62. The Second Circuit found that the probative value of Black's testimony was outweighed by its potential for unfair prejudice under Federal Rule of Evidence 403. *See id.* The Second Circuit also faulted the trial court for receiving in evidence a videotape of the Yemen wedding, at which a Hamas leader referred to the Tel Aviv bombing, and for admitting certain documents seized in Croatia from two Yemenis who were crossing from Bosnia into Croatia. *See id.* at 157, 175-76. The court found that some of these items were hearsay. *See id.*

[54] *Available at* http://www.usdoj.gov/opa/pr/2009/January/09-nsd-041.html.

[55] Separately, al-Delaema pled guilty to one count of aggravated assault for a December 2007 incident in which he kicked a prison guard to the point of unconsciousness. As part of his plea agreement, al-Delaema stipulated to an eighteen-month sentence on the assault charge. *See* Plea Agreement,

United States v. al-Delaema, No. 05-cr-00337 (D.D.C. Feb. 26, 2009) (Dkt. No. 92); *see also* Press Release, U.S. Dep't of Justice, Iraqi-Born Dutch Citizen Pleads Guilty to Terrorism Conspiracy Against Americans in Iraq (Feb. 26, 2009), *available at* http://www.usdoj.gov/opa/pr/2009/February/09-nsd-168.html.

[56] *Available at* http://abcnews.go.com/US/wireStory?id=7343765.

[57] *Available at* http://washingtondc.fbi.gov/dojpressrel/pressrel09/wfo041609.htm.

[58] *Online version available at* http://www.nytimes.com/2009/05/24/us/politics/24gitmo.html.

[59] *Available at* 2009 WLNR 4814238.

[60] *Available at* http://phoenix.bizjournals.com/phoenix/stories/2009/02/09/daily27.html.

[61] *Available at* http://www.nypost.com/seven/01232009/news/politics/the_terrorists_will_now_cheer_151497.htm.

[62] *Online version available at* http://www.nytimes.com/2009/05/21/us/politics/21detain.html.

[63] *Available at* http://www.usdoj.gov/opa/pr/2009/June/09-ag-563.html.

[64] *Available at* http://www.usdoj.gov/opa/pr/2009/June/09-ag-564.html.

[65] The release also states that "[i]n addition to those inmates with an international terrorism history or nexus, there are approximately 139 individuals in BOP custody who have a history of/or nexus to domestic terrorism," including individuals like Theodore Kaczynski, the Unabomber, and Terry Nichols, convicted for his part in the 1995 Oklahoma City bombing. Press Release, U.S. Dep't of Justice, Fact Sheet: Prosecuting and Detaining Terror Suspects in the U.S. Criminal Justice System; *see also* Solomon Moore, *Doubts on Handling Terror Detainees End at U.S. Prison Gates*, N.Y. Times, June 17, 2009, at A14, *online version available at* http://www.nytimes.com/2009/06/17/us/17victorville.html (discussing fact that no international terrorist has escaped from any part of the federal prison system and that prison officials believe they can handle such prisoners).

[66] The release states that "[a]s of May 22, 2009, there were 44 inmates subject to SAMs, out of a total federal inmate population of more than 205,000" and that out of those forty-four, twenty-nine were incarcerated on terrorism-related charges, while eleven were either gang or organized crime members, and four were incarcerated on espionage charges. Press Release, U.S. Dep't of Justice, Fact Sheet: Prosecuting and Detaining Terror Suspects in the U.S. Criminal Justice System. We discussed SAMs at some length in *In Pursuit of Justice*. See *In Pursuit of Justice*, at 124-27.

www.ingramcontent.com/pod-product-compliance
Lightning Source LLC
Chambersburg PA
CBHW051422200326

41520CB00023B/7333